FROM PAIN TO EMPOWERMENT:

A TEEN'S GUIDE TO BREAK FREE FROM TOXIC RELATIONSHIPS, REBUILD CONFIDENCE, AND EMBRACE SELF-LOVE

JORDAN PHOENIX

Copyright Page

DISCLAIMER

This book is intended to provide educational information on the topics it covers. The author and the publisher are not providing medical, psychological, or therapeutic advice. The content of this book is not intended to be a substitute for professional medical advice, diagnosis, or treatment. Always seek the advice of your physician or other qualified health providers with any questions you may have regarding a medical condition or mental health concerns.

The stories, experiences, and advice presented in this book are based on the author's research and personal insights. They are provided as guidance and to foster understanding and empathy, not as definitive medical or psychological advice. The author and publisher disclaim any liability, loss, or risk, personal or otherwise, which is incurred as a consequence, directly or indirectly, of the use and application of any of the contents of this book.

Given the sensitive nature of the topics discussed, some content may be triggering or unsettling for young readers. Adults are encouraged to preview the material and use their discretion when sharing it with children or adolescents.

If you or someone you know is in immediate danger or needs urgent help, please contact a trusted adult, healthcare professional, or the appropriate emergency services number in your country.

CONTENTS

INTRODUCTION

Hey there! I'm really glad you're here, holding this book. It tells me you're looking for answers, maybe trying to figure out some tough stuff about relationships. It's okay if you're feeling confused, hurt, or even a bit scared. It's okay if you're not even sure what's up with your relationship. That's exactly why this book exists.

See, sometimes relationships get twisted up in ways that make us feel really bad. You might feel like everything's your fault or like you can't do anything right. Maybe you're being put down, hurt, or just feeling lost. It's tough, especially when you're not sure why it's happening or what to do about it.

This book is here to help you see things clearly. It's about under- standing what a healthy relationship should feel like and recog- nizing when something's not right. We'll talk about things like gaslighting, red flags, abuse, manipulation, control, and all those warning signs that something's off.

But more than that, this book is about you. It's about helping you realize that you're not the problem. It's about showing you that you deserve to be treated with kindness, respect, and love. And it's about giving you the tools to help you move forward, whether that means getting out of a bad situation or healing from one.

So, take a deep breath. You're not alone in this. You're taking a big step just by reading these words. Let's walk through this together, okay? You've got this. And remember, no matter how things might feel right now, you're worthy of a happy, healthy relationship. Let's start this journey.

TRIGGER WARNING

Before you dive into this book, there's something really important I need to share with you. This isn't your average book. We're going to explore some pretty heavy stuff – things like abuse, trauma, and all sorts of experiences that might be tough to read about.

A Heads-Up on What's Inside: We're going to talk about different kinds of abuse, including physical and emotional abuse and even sexual abuse. It's real talk, with real stories and situations. The goal here isn't to make you uncomfortable; it's to help, to educate, and to empower. But sometimes, to get there, we have to go through some dark and difficult topics. It's important stuff, but it can also be really challenging.

Take Care of You: If at any point you feel overwhelmed, anxious, or just need a break, please, please take it. This book isn't going anywhere, and you can always come back to it when you're ready. Your well-being is the most important thing.

Who This Book Is For: If you've had experiences with toxic relationships, abuse, or trauma, or if you're just curious about these topics, this book is for you. But if you find these topics particularly triggering, it's totally okay to skip this one. You know yourself best.

A Reminder: This book is here to support and guide you, but it's not a substitute for professional help. If you're struggling, reaching out to a counselor, therapist, or a trusted adult can be a really brave and important step.

So, with all that said, if you're ready, let's step into this journey together. It might be tough at times, but I believe in you and your strength to get through it. You're not alone in this – we're in it together.

1

UNMASKING THE FACES OF TOXICITY

Yo, welcome to the first step of understanding this whole 'toxic relationship' maze.

This chapter's all about giving you the 411 on what makes a rela- tionship toxic, so you can spot the red flags before things

go south. Remember, it's totally okay to bail on a relationship that's messing with your happiness and peace of mind.

And hey, if you're feeling stuck in a relationship that's more 'ugh' than 'aww,' don't worry. It's something that tons of people go through all over the world. Did you know that 26% of girls and 15% of guys have been in an abusive relationship before they even hit 18? That's a lot of us dealing with some heavy stuff. It doesn't matter who you are – this stuff can happen to anyone.

But the big question is, how do you spot it? How do you figure out when something that started as so cool and exciting turns into something... not so great?

Do you feel like you're riding a rollercoaster of emotions?

At first, you're all giddy with those awesome butterflies in your stomach, texting non-stop and sneaking cute glances at each other across the room. It's like your heart's doing back-flips! But then, out of nowhere, things start to shift. Those butterflies turn into heavy knots, texts become less sweet and more sour, and those glances? They start to feel like someone's constantly watching you and disapproving.

So, what's the real deal with toxic relationships? Let's unmask this bad boy.

More Than Just a Buzzword: 'Toxic' is a word that gets tossed around a lot, but it's super serious when it comes to relationships. It's not just about having a bad day; it's about a pattern of behavior that makes you feel worse, not better.

What Toxic Really Looks Like: Imagine a relationship where you're always feeling drained, emotionally and mentally. Like, every time you're with them, you end up feeling down or stressed. That's the hallmark of a toxic relationship. It's not just arguments (which happen in every relationship); it's about feeling controlled, manipulated, or constantly criticized.

The Many Masks of Toxicity: Toxicity can show up in different outfits – like that partner who's always on your case, criticizing everything from your friends to your fashion choices. Or maybe they're never there for you emotionally, making you feel like you're talking to a wall. And let's not forget about the green-eyed monster, jealousy, which can turn from cute to controlling really quickly.

Not Your Typical Ups and Downs: A toxic relationship is like an emotional vampire. It sucks the life out of you, leaving you feeling drained, both in your heart and your head. We're talking about a whole pattern of bad vibes: abuse, manipulation, and control. These aren't your everyday arguments. This is next-level nega- tivity that does more harm than good.

It's important to recognize that these behaviors – the control, the manipulation, the constant negativity – they're not normal. They're signs of a relationship that's hurting and not helping your mental and emotional well-being.

LET'S BREAK DOWN ABUSE AND TOXICITY IN RELATIONSHIPS

So, we're diving into something super important here – under- standing abuse in relationships. It's more than just physical; it comes in different forms, each messed up in its own way. Let's unpack this, so you know what to watch out for.

Emotional/Psychological Abuse: The Mind Games

This kind of abuse is all about messing with your head and heart. It's like when someone insults you, threatens you, or plays mind games (yeah, that gaslighting stuff). It's sneaky because it's not always in-your-face, but it totally wrecks your emotional well- being.

Picture this: There's that one person who always finds something to criticize about you. "Why do you wear that?" "You're not going to eat that, are you?" "Stop listening to that music." It's like nothing you do is ever good enough. That's a red flag waving right in your face.

Or maybe there's someone who's about as emotionally available as a brick wall. You're pouring your heart out, and they're just scrolling through their phone. Feels pretty lonely, right?

And then there's jealousy – but not the cute, slightly annoying kind. We're talking extreme, over-the-top jealousy. Like, they get mad if you even talk to someone of the opposite gender or smile at the cashier. It's not just insecurity; it's possessiveness, and that's not cool.

Physical Abuse: The Hurtful Touch

Physical abuse is straight-up violence – hitting, pushing, stran- gling, kicking, pinching, any kind of physical harm.

It's not just about bruises or scars; it's about someone using force to control you. And, threatening to hit you also counts!

Sexual Abuse: Crossing Boundaries

This one's about forcing or pressuring someone into sexual stuff they're not cool with. It's not just physical; it can be verbal too, like sexual comments that make you feel gross and violated. Forcing you to take nude pics. Sharing your secrets or pics with others.

Violating your privacy. Or telling nasty lies about sexual things you didn't do.

Digital Abuse: The Tech Terror

In our always-online world, digital abuse is a big deal. It's using tech – like constant texts, asking you where you are and what you're doing, demanding to know passwords, or cyberbullying – to control or scare someone. Think of it as digital handcuffs.

Remember, it's super important to know that this stuff isn't normal. Sure, every relationship has its ups and downs – that's just life. But a toxic relationship? That's like being on a rollercoaster that only goes down. It's like being stuck in a maze where every turn is just another dead end of drama. Full of never-ending stress and sadness.

So, here's the bottom line: You deserve to be in a relationship that lifts you up, not one that drags you down. If you're feeling more drained than energized, more criticized than supported, it's time to take a step back and think, "Is this really what I want?"

Knowing about these types of abuse is key to spotting them. Each one is serious and can really mess with someone's life. Understanding this stuff is like putting on armor; it helps you protect yourself and others from getting hurt in these toxic ways. Stay informed, stay safe.

In the next sections, we'll dive even deeper. We'll talk about how to spot these toxic traits and, most importantly, how to deal with them. It's all about taking care of you, because you're the main character in your story. Stay tuned!

SPOTTING THE RED FLAGS

Okay, so getting wise to the early signs of a toxic relationship is like learning to dodge a bullet. Seriously, spotting these red flags early can save you a ton of emotional pain and heartache down the road.

The Give-and-Take Imbalance: Ever feel like you're the only one putting effort into your relationship? Like, you're always the one making plans, sending texts, showing love, but getting zilch in return? That's a major red flag. A healthy relationship is a two-way street, not a one-person show.

Feeling Small, Not Tall: If your partner's making you feel like you're less – less smart, less cool, less anything – that's not okay. In a good relationship, your partner should be your cheerleader, not someone who makes you feel like you can't do anything right.

Walking on Eggshells: This one's a biggie. If you're constantly worrying about setting your partner off, or if you're always tiptoeing around to avoid conflict, that's a sign things aren't healthy. You should feel comfy and safe in your relationship, not like you're stepping through a minefield.

OTHER SIGNS TO WATCH OUT FOR

But wait, there's more. Toxic relationships can have a whole bunch of different red flags:

Abusive Behavior: This one's serious. If there's any kind of physi- cal, emotional, or verbal abuse going on (hitting, bruising, slap- ping, insulting, yelling), that's a massive red flag. Abuse is never okay, no matter what.

Control Freak Much? If your partner's trying to control what you wear, who you hang out with, or even what you post on Insta, that's not about love; it's about control. When someone's always checking up on you, invading your privacy, and micro-managing your life, it's def toxic.

It starts small: they want to know who you're texting or why you're late. Then, it escalates: they start dictating how you should look, whom you should be friends with, what hobbies you should have, or even what you should eat. They mask it as concern or love, but it's not. It's about control. It's about them wanting to dictate your life, your choices, your freedom. It's as if you're living in a cage, and they're the ones holding the key.

Where Did My Freedom Go?

Ever feel like you're living your life, but someone else is calling the shots? If your partner's always making decisions for you, that's a red flag. It's like you're a character in their story, not the main character in yours. You should be able to make your own choices, big or small. It's your life, after all!

Crazy Jealousy: Your partner gets upset if you talk to someone of the opposite gender. They question your loyalty because of an innocent social media interaction. They see threats where there are none. This type of jealousy is not about love; it's about posses- sion. Extreme jealousy, like demanding you unfollow certain people or show your messages – that shows their insecurity, not love.

Trust is the foundation of a healthy relationship, and without it, things can get really shaky.

Cutting You Off: Isolating you from friends, controlling who you meet – that's a tactic to keep you all to themselves.

Ever feel like your partner's trying to build a world where it's just the two of you? They might try to turn your friends and family against you or make you feel guilty for spending time with them. Isolating you from your support system is a tactic to make you more dependent on them, which is totally unhealthy.

- **Manipulating Your Connections**: Spreading lies or creating drama to cause rifts between you and your loved ones.
- **Making You Choose**: Saying things like, "If you really loved me, you'd spend more time with me," to make you feel guilty.
- **Moving Away from Your Support**: Suggesting moving far away or living together super early to distance you from your friends and family.

Cold Shoulder Games: Stonewalling, ghosting, or suddenly going cold is a way to mess with your head. It's a tactic to make you feel insecure and obey them in order to get them to be loving again.

Over-the-Top Love Bombing: Too much too fast can be a sign of trying to hook you quickly and deeply.

The 'You Owe Me' Line: If they keep reminding you of what they've done for you to get their way, it's manipulative.

Wild Mood Swings: Unpredictable moods can create a tense and unstable environment.

Emotional Blackmail: Making you feel guilty or scared to influ- ence your actions. Threatening self-harm or to harm you if you don't do what they want? Definitely toxic.

Blame Game: When it's always "your fault," that's a way to avoid taking responsibility.

The 'No One Else' Threat: "No one else will love you" – that's a classic line to make you feel trapped.

Insults Disguised as Jokes: Sometimes, toxic partners will throw insults at you and then brush them off as 'just joking.' But if those 'jokes' make you feel bad, they're not funny.

Selfishness Overload: If it's all about them – their problems, their feelings, their wants – and never about you, that's not a partner- ship; it's a one-person show with you as the audience.

Never Feeling Good Enough: If you're constantly made to feel like you're not smart, pretty, or cool enough, that's a big no-no.

The Misery Mix: Yelling, insulting, any form of hurting you – these are all signs of a toxic vibe.

Flirt Alert: If your guy is constantly flirting with other girls, even when you're right there, that's a major red flag. It can leave you feeling like you're not enough or that he's not really into you. And if he's talking about other girls in a way that makes you uncom- fortable, that's not cool either. A committed partner should make you feel secure, not jealous or second-best.

Crossing the Line: Big one here. If your boyfriend is pres- suring you to get physical before you're ready, or if he's pushing you to do things that make you feel uncomfortable or even downright miser- able, that's a huge no-no. Your body, your rules. Period.

Peer Pressure Turned Up: Whether it's alcohol, drugs, or anything else, if your partner is pressuring you to partake and then mocks or manipulates you when you say no, that's toxic behavior. Standing your ground on what you put into your body is impor-

tant, and anyone who tries to sway you otherwise doesn't have your best interests at heart.

Absolute Deal-Breaker: If he ever hits you or even threatens to, that's more than a red flag – it's a stop sign. Physical abuse is never, ever okay. It's dangerous and a clear sign that you need to get out of that situation ASAP.

The Emotional Rollercoaster: If one minute he's all loving and attentive and the next he's cold as ice, leaving you wondering where you stand. That's not stability – that's a mind game. Consistency is key in a healthy relationship; you shouldn't have to live in a constant state of confusion about his feelings for you.

Jealousy and Isolation: If he gets super jealous and tries to isolate you from your friends or family, that's a sign of control, not love.

Gaslighting: If you find yourself questioning your reality because he's twisting the truth or denying things that

happened, that's gaslighting – a form of emotional manipulation.

Constant Blame Game: If he never takes responsibility for
his actions and always blames you for everything, that's not
just unfair, it's unhealthy.

Phew! That's a lot, isn't it?

These behaviors are all about control, and they can make you
feel trapped, like you're losing your identity. It's important to
recog- nize these signs and understand that this isn't what a
healthy rela- tionship looks like.

You deserve to be in a relationship where you feel free,
respected, and trusted. If you find yourself in this situation,
don't be afraid to reach out for help. Talk to someone you
trust, set boundaries, and remember, your feelings and
freedom matter. You're not alone, and you have the strength
to seek a healthier, happier path.

Always remember, you're the author of your own story, and
you get to decide who's in it and how they treat you. Stay
true to your- self, and never settle for a relationship that
makes you feel less than amazing.

Well friends, that's the lowdown on spotting the red flags in
a rela- tionship. Stay alert, stay strong, and remember, you
deserve to be treated with love and respect!

You got this!

HEALTHY VS. TOXIC: KNOWING THE DIFFERENCE

Now, let's contrast this with what healthy relationships look like:

1. **Trust vs. Suspicion**: In a good relationship, there's trust and comfort, not constant doubt.
2. **Honesty vs. Lies**: Being honest, even when it's hard, is key to a healthy relationship.
3. **Your Own Identity**: You should be able to have your own friends, hobbies, and time. You don't have to lose yourself in the relationship.
4. **Independence vs. Dependence**: Being able to stand on your own two feet is healthy; being forced to obey and depend on someone else, not so much.
5. **Feeling Happy vs. Unhappy**: A healthy relationship makes you feel happy and at ease, not constantly tense.
6. **Accepting Each Other**: It's about loving each other as you are, not trying to mold each other into something else.
7. **Encouragement vs Put-Downs**: Your partner should be your cheerleader, not your critic.
8. **Feeling Safe vs Endangered**: You should feel safe and secure, not scared or on edge.

Wrapping It Up

Knowing the difference between healthy and unhealthy rela-tion- ships is like having a roadmap for your heart. Keep these signs in mind as you navigate your relationships. Remember, you deserve a love that lifts you up, respects you, and makes you feel good about who you are.

You're worthy of a relationship that's built on trust, respect, and genuine care. Stay aware, stay true to yourself, and never settle for less than you deserve. You got this!

TOXIC TYPES OF PARTNERS – THE " NEVER DATE" LIST

Heads Up: Some People Are Just Bad News

Alright, let's get real about the types of people you should avoid dating. Trust me, steering clear of these types can save you a whole lot of heartache and drama.

The Red Flag Roster

1. **The Aggressor**: If they have a history of getting into fights or hitting people, that's a massive red flag. Aggressive behavior can easily turn into abuse.
2. **Mr. or Ms. Flirty-Flirt**: If they're super flirty with everyone, even when they're with you, or if they've got a history of cheating, beware. If they cheated with you, chances are they might cheat on you too.

3. **The Liar**: Little white lies here and there are one thing, but if they're all about spinning tall tales and not being truthful, that's a no-go. Trust is key in a relationship, and with a liar, you'll never have that.

4. **The Controller**: If they're always trying to tell you what to do, what to wear, who to hang out with – that's controlling behavior, and it's totally unhealthy.

5. **The Guilt-Tripper**: This person is all about making you feel guilty for... well, pretty much everything, even their own problems! They use guilt to manipulate and control you.

6. **The Jealous Type**: A little jealousy can be normal, but if they're constantly suspicious or accusing you of things you didn't do, that's a sign of insecurity and possessiveness.

7. **The Mind-Game Player**: If you feel like you're in a psychological thriller every time you're with them because of their mind games, it's time to walk away.

8. **The Bad-Mouther**: If they're always talking trash about their exes or other people, that's a sign of disrespect. Chances are, they'll talk about you the same way.

Why These Types Are Bad News

Dating someone with these traits can make you feel miserable, insecure, and even scared. A relationship should be about support, love, and respect, not stress, fear, and drama.

Trust Your Gut

Remember, if something feels off about someone you're dating, trust your instincts. You deserve someone who treats you well and makes you feel valued and happy, not someone who brings a truckload of toxicity into your life.

So, keep these types in mind, and if you spot them, run the other way. You're worth so much more than a toxic relationship. Stay smart, stay strong, and remember, the right person will make you feel good, not bad.

TOXIC RELATIONSHIP STORIES

Reading these stories can help you realize you're not alone – and that the problem is not YOU; it's THEM.

Emily's Story

"jake was the coolest boy in class. when i started dating Jake i felt like i was on top of the world. but things changed... slowly at first. he'd make comments about my friends, saying they were lame, telling me not to hang with them and I started seeing them less. then he'd get mad if I spent time with anyone but him. i remember this one time he scrolled through my Instagram and started deleting pictures he didnt like!! just like he owned me and my accounts! it felt like he was erasing parts of me. i became this

girl I didnt recognize – always anxious, always trying to please
him. and no matter how hard i tried i was never good enough for
him. he was never happy with me. my confidence plummeted. i
felt trapped but i thought thats what love was supposed to be like
right?

Eventually i couldnt take it and left him. it was SOOOO hard to
leave him i thought i wouldn't survive... but i did! now im with a
really loving guy. hes the best ever! he never insults me or tells me
what to do or who to hang with. we laugh a lot and have so much!
im so glad I left Jake."

Red Flags: Control Alert

Jake's vibe of cutting Emily off from her squad and taking over her social life? Major red flag. It's like emotional hijacking, trying to control who she chills with. And yo, him deleting her Insta pics without asking? Total invasion of her space. It's like he's trying to edit her life and who she is.

Jake always being down on everything Emily does is like an energy vampire, sucking out all her good vibes and self-confidence. Not cool.

Healthy Behavior: The Real Deal

In a healthy relationship, it's all about cheering on each other's independence. Think supporting their friendships, not crashing the party. It's about being their fan, not their director.

Partners who get it right? They respect each other's digital lives, too. No password policing or social media sabotage. Decisions? Made together, with respect.

A partner who's really in your corner? They celebrate your efforts, not nitpick. They're about lifting you up, not dragging you down.

Jay

"When you flipped out and snapped at me, I kinda thought, 'Is something wrong with me?' But then, like a lightbulb moment, I got it. Your anger was just showing how messed up you were, not me. And just like that, I knew I was okay. I was cool, but not with you hanging around."

— JAY

Red Flags: Temper Trouble

Getting super mad and blowing up? That's a signal of not handling emotions in a healthy way. It's like a storm that leaves everyone soaked and miserable.

Healthy communication is like a chill convo – it's about sharing feelings, not shouting. It's listening, understanding, and working through stuff together, not dumping your bad vibes on the other person.

Healthy Behavior: Cool Calmness

In a relationship that's got it going on, both peeps own their feel- ings. No blame games. They tackle issues like a team, not like opponents in a boxing ring.

Zoe's Awakening

"When I first got with Marcus, I thought his jealousy was kinda cute. Like, he really cares, right? Wrong. He'd freak if I even talked to other guys. It was like being under constant surveillance. I'd make excuses for him, telling myself he's just protective. But deep down, I knew. I was losing myself, becoming this girl who was scared to speak up, scared to make him mad. I was tense, afraid to trigger his anger fits. I felt scared, all day, every day. My once bubbly personality? Gone. I was becoming a shadow of my old self."

Red Flags: Green-Eyed Monster

Marcus's jealousy level? Over the top. Him freaking out over Zoe talking to other guys screams control, not care. It's like a warning siren for worse things.

Feeling watched 24/7 by your partner is more prison guard than guardian angel. And Zoe losing her spark? That's what happens when you're living in fear, not love.

Healthy Behavior: Trust and Cheer

Now, flip the script to a healthy scene. It's built on trust, not tracking devices. Partners feel secure, not suspicious.

A partner who's really rooting for you? They're your personal hype team, celebrating what makes you amazing. No dimming your shine.

Real love is like mutual respect – it's feeling safe to be yourself, always. No walking on eggshells, just walking on sunshine.

Hannah's Hard Lesson

"Liam is the hottest boy in school. I was SO excited when he started dating me.

At first he'd tell me how amazing I was... but then he started to change slowly. He'd say hurtful things, little digs at first, about how I dressed or how I laughed too loud. 'You sound like a horse' he told me once when I laughed about a joke. Another time, 'You look like shit' when I wore a new pair of jeans. He started telling me what to eat and wear. I did everything to make him happy. I started to change, bit by bit, hoping to be his 'perfect girl.' But nothing was ever 'pretty enough' or good enough for him.

the more I changed, the less I felt like Hannah. I was fading away. I'd look in the mirror and not recognize the girl staring back. It was like he'd stolen my light, and all that was left was this dim, depressed version of me."

Red Flags Alert

Harsh Words, Harsh Vibes: Liam's comments about Hannah's laugh and clothes? Total verbal put-downs. Being mean about the things that make Hannah, well, Hannah, is majorly not cool.

Control Freak Alert: Liam telling Hannah what to eat and wear? Big red flag. It's like he's trying to turn her into someone she's not, and that's all about control, not care.

Never Good Enough: Nothing Hannah does is ever right in Liam's eyes. That's like an endless downer, chipping away at her self-love and turning her sparkle into a fizzle.

Healthy Behavior Goals

Respect and Love the Real You: In a healthy relationship, your partner digs your laugh, your style, all the things that are uniquely you. They're about lifting you up, not dressing you down.

Your Style, Your Choice: A partner who's really got your back? They love your vibe, whatever it is. They're not about giving you a makeover to suit their style.

Cheerleader, Not Critic: A good partner is your personal cheer squad. They see your efforts, they cheer for you, not make you feel small or unworthy.

Sarah's Story

"Okay, so about Alex. He was charming, like prince charming, but with a dark side. He'd snap over the smallest things. One minute we're all good, the next, he's a raging storm, throwing insults like they were nothing.

I used to be this happy confident girl. But with him, I turned into a little mouse. I would flinch whenever he raised his voice and do anything to please him. But here's the thing: I woke up. I realized this wasn't love; it was control. It took everything I had, but I walked away. And guess what? I found my spark again."

Red Flags Spotted

Temper Tantrums: Alex flipping out over tiny stuff? That's like living with a ticking time bomb. Total mood killer and super scary.

Mouse Transformation: Sarah going from confident to super timid around Alex? That's a sign of feeling intimidated, and that's a big no-no for a healthy relationship.

Voiceless and Scared: Feeling scared to speak up or stand your ground? That's not love, that's being silenced. Not what relation- ships are about.

Healthy Relationship Real Talk

Chill Vibes Only: In a cool relationship, small stuff stays small. No over-the-top reactions, just calm chats and under- standing.

Confidence Booster: A fab partner makes you feel more you, not less. They're about boosting your confidence, not busting it.

Feel Safe, Be Heard: Feeling safe to say what's on your

mind? That's relationship goals. It's all about mutual respect, where your voice matters just as much as theirs.

Becky's Story

Becky: I have brown eyes. every time my boyfriend sees a girl with blue eyes he points her out and says "Wow what beautiful eyes she has!" He longingly says how he wishes to have a blue-eyed girlfriend, how much prettier that is, what a dream that would be. it makes me feel like I just can't be pretty enough for him.

Red Flags, for Real

Eye-Color Obsession: Becky's boyfriend going gaga over blue eyes in front of her? That's like a direct hit to her self-esteem. Making someone feel less-than because of their looks? Super shallow.

Dream Girl Diss: Him talking about wanting a blue-eyed girl- friend is like saying Becky's not his dream girl. That's a big ouch on the heart and totally not okay.

What's Up with Healthy Love?

Love the Eyes You Look Into: In a happy, healthy relationship, it's about loving the person you're with – brown eyes, blue eyes, what- ever. It's about seeing the beauty in them, not wishing for some- thing else.

Appreciate, Don't Compare: A partner who's truly into you isn't comparing you to some fantasy. They're all about appreciating the real, amazing person in front of them.

Jill's Story

Jill: *"my boyfriend says I'm stupid, useless, and ugly. he says he's the only idiot who would ever stick around with me. and if I leave him no one else will ever love me. I feel so awful unlovable and so afraid he'll leave. What to do?"*

Jill, first off, I want to say that what your boyfriend is telling you? It's not only untrue, but it's also really hurtful and unfair. Calling you names and saying he's the only one who would stick around is a classic case of emotional manipulation. He's trying to make you feel worthless so that you'll feel dependent on him. But here's the truth: you're not stupid, useless, or ugly. You're a valuable, beau- tiful person with so much to offer. And absolutely, someone else will love and appreciate the real you. Remember, no one has the right to make you feel bad about yourself, especially not someone who's supposed to care about you.

Kate's Story

Kate: *"my boyfriend has this thing where every time after we eat together (pizza, donuts, whatever) he then looks at me and says "you're going to be such a disgusting fat pig soon! you're already getting fatter every day. you*

shouldn't have eaten that." and then he laughs and says he's joking and I'm too serious and can't take a joke. it makes me feel awful. I dread eating with him but he says if I don't then that means I don't love him. I don't know what to do. Advice?"

Kate, I'm really sorry you're going through this. When your boyfriend makes those comments about your eating and your body, it's not just a 'joke.' It's body shaming, and it's not okay. How it makes you feel is important and valid. Eating should be a joyful, guilt-free experience, not something you dread. And you should never feel forced to do something to 'prove' your love. Love is about acceptance and kindness, not criticism and control. You deserve to be with someone who makes you feel good about your- self, who loves you for who you are, not someone who puts you down.

Rosanna's Story

Rosanna: my boyfriend said he likes girls with big breasts and keeps telling me I have such miserable little ones. I caught him watching porn with girls with big cleavage and he said he is the "unlucky bastard stuck with a skinny little girl"

Rosanna, hearing what your boyfriend says about your body must be really tough. But here's something super important: his prefer- ences and comments do not define your worth or beauty. Your body is yours, and it's perfect just the way it is. Watching certain types of content and then comparing you to it is not only unfair but also incredibly disrespectful. It's okay to feel hurt by this, and it's okay to stand up for your- self. You deserve someone who loves and respects you as you are, who finds you beautiful without any conditions or comparisons. Remember, you are enough, just as you are.

And that's the scoop on these relationship red flags vs. the healthy stuff. Remember, a relationship should make you feel awesome, not less. Keep your eyes open for the good vibes and ditch the bad ones. You deserve the best!

EXAMPLES OF HAPPY RELATIONSHIPS

Maya's Relationship

"I remember when I first started dating Leo, I was worried we'd lose ourselves in the relationship. But it was different with him. He'd encourage me to hang out with my friends and pursue my hobbies. We had this beautiful balance of being together and having our own space.

He'd listen – like, really listen – when I talked about my dreams. And he'd share his too. We respected each other's boundaries and supported each other's goals. It felt like we were not just lovers but best friends, growing together but also as individuals."

Jasmine's Relationship

"When I met Ryan, I had just come out of a pretty rough relation-ship. I was scared to open up again. But Ryan, he was patient. He understood my need for taking things slow and never pushed me beyond my comfort zone.

We built our relationship on mutual respect and trust. He showed me what it means to be truly loved and valued. We could talk for hours or sit in comfortable silence. It was like a breath of fresh air, a gentle and understanding love that healed rather than hurt."

Ava's Relationship

"Ron and I, we're like a team. We tackle everything together – the good, the bad, and the ugly. When I'm stressed about school or family stuff, he's my rock, always there to lend an ear or give a comforting hug.

What I love most is how we celebrate each other's successes. When I won the art competition, he was cheering the loudest. It's not just about being in love; it's about being in a true partnership where you lift each other up every single day."

Ellie's Story

"Being with Bruce taught me what respect really means in a relationship. He always considers my feelings and opinions, and we make decisions together. It's never about one person calling all the shots.

We've had our disagreements, sure, but we handle them with maturity. We talk things out, listen to each other, and find a middle ground. It's a relationship where I feel heard, valued, and genuinely loved. With Bruce, I've learned that love is about giving respect as much as it is about receiving it."

THE CYCLE OF ABUSE: PREDICTABLE LIKE A STORM

The Unpredictable Predictability of Abusers

Hey, did you know that abusers are kinda like weather patterns? You can almost predict what they'll do next, just like forecasting a storm. It's weird, right? Even if you think your situation is unique, it's probably more typical than you think.

Understanding the Abuse Cycle

The cycle of abuse is like a never-ending loop of bad weather:

1. The Tension Building Phase: The Brewing Storm

It's like the air before a storm – tense, heavy. Kinda like a storm's about to hit. It's all about escalating tensions, where the littlest things set off major drama. You're walking in a minefield, doing everything to keep things chill and avoid setting off your partner. That's the tension building phase – where you're on high alert, waiting for the storm to break.

2. The Incident: This is the storm hitting – the abuse itself. It can be physical, emotional, verbal... just plain nasty. Lighting strikes. This is when things turn ugly, and your partner's anger explodes, whether it's yelling, blaming, or worse. It's sudden, intense, and scary. You're left shocked and hurt, trying to make sense of what just happened.

3. **Reconciliation**: After the storm, there's the calm. They might apologize, promise to change, shower you with love and gifts. It's like the sun peeking out after a tornado.

Your partner's all sorry, promising to change, and being super sweet. It's like they're a totally different person, and you start thinking maybe things will get better. They're saying all the right things, and for a moment, you want to believe that it's all going to be okay.

4. **Calm: The eye of the storm**: Things seem okay for a bit. It's peaceful, and you start to think maybe it's over. It's like your part- ner's acting as if nothing bad happened. Every-thing seems normal, and you start questioning if it was all in your head. But deep down, you know it's like the eye of a hurricane – calm but not really safe.

And then, the tension starts building again... and it repeats itself! Over and over.

The Hope Trap

You might hope that this time it'll be different, that they'll change. But here's the harsh truth: they won't. This cycle? It tends to repeat itself, and staying in it, hoping for a brighter dawn, usually just leads to more storms.

The Psychological Impact of Toxic Relationships

Being in a toxic relationship can really mess with your head. It's like carrying around a heavy backpack of bad feelings all the time.

- **Mental Health**: You might feel constantly anxious, depressed, or even scared.
- **Self-Esteem**: Your confidence takes a hit. You start believing you're not good enough.
- **Well-Being**: You lose touch with what makes you happy. It's like you're stuck under a dark cloud.
- **Negative Beliefs**: You might start believing things like "I'm not worthy of love" or "I can't do anything right."
- **Limiting Beliefs**: These are beliefs that hold you back, like "I'll never find someone better" or "I deserve this."
- **Common Emotional Responses**: Feeling guilty, ashamed, helpless, or even numb.

Breaking Free

Realizing you're in this cycle is the first step to breaking out of it. It's tough, but remember, you deserve a relationship that's sunny more than it's stormy. You deserve respect, love, and happiness.

Don't be afraid to reach out for help – to friends, family,

coun- selors. Set boundaries, focus on what's best for you, and slowly find the strength to say 'enough is enough.'

There's a whole world outside this storm, and you deserve to expe- rience it. You're stronger than you think, and you've got this!

Stepping Off the Ride: Breaking the Cycle

Breaking free from this cycle isn't easy, but it's like starting your own personal revolution. It's about seeing the pattern, under- standing what's happening, and deciding you deserve better.

When you finally step off this toxic merry-go-round, you're not just escaping the cycle, you're stepping into a new chapter of self- care, healing, and empowerment. That's the moment you start moving towards a life where you're in control, where you're valued, and where you're truly free.

Remember, you deserve a life filled with respect, love, and happi- ness, not one stuck in a cycle of pain and confusion. Trust in your- self, reach out for help, and take that brave step towards a brighter, healthier future. You've got this!

"A M I IN A TOXIC REL ATIONSHIP?" QUIZ

Time for Some Real Talk

Let's dive into some questions that might shed light on your rela- tionship. Answer honestly – this is all about helping you under- stand your situation better.

Fill-in-the-Blank: Your Feelings with Your Partner

1. "When I'm with my partner, I feel ."
2. "Before this relationship, I used to feel ."
3. "In this relationship, I feel like I am/am not the same person because ."
4. "I feel like I'm a to my partner."
5. "I feel like my partner me."

Understanding Your Relationship

It's important to understand where you stand in your rela- tionship. Are you being treated with respect and love, or are you feeling down and controlled? Remember, you deserve a relationship that makes you feel good about yourself, where you can be your true self.

Reflecting on Your Thoughts

Look back at your quiz answers. If you're seeing signs of feeling controlled, belittled, ashamed of who you are, or not yourself, it might be time to rethink your relationship. You're worth more than toxic treatment – you deserve real, healthy love.

Always remember, it's okay to seek help and talk to someone you trust. Understanding these factors can help you make informed decisions about your relationship. You're not alone in this, and there's always a way to a healthier, happier you. You got this!

2

EMOTIONAL ABUSE

UNRAVELING EMOTIONAL ABUSE

Emotional abuse isn't always loud or obvious. Sometimes, it's sneaky, but it always leaves scars. This chapter will help you understand if you're in an unhealthy relationship and the various

tactics that might be used against you.

Here's a rundown of what it can look like:

Hurtful Words: Insults about your looks, skills, intelligence, dreams - anything that can make you feel small and insignif-icant. It could be telling you you're stupid, ugly, too thin, too fat, worth- less, useless, good for nothing, a loser, not pretty enough, etc.

Belittling: Regularly questioning or doubting your intelligence or capabilities, such as "Are you sure you can handle that? You usually mess things up." Or "I wouldn't trust you to do that, you're not smart enough."

Dismissive Comments: Brushing off your thoughts, feelings, or achievements as unimportant or trivial. For instance, responding to your accomplishment with "That's nothing special" or "Anyone could have done that."

Undermining Achievements: Diminishing or negating your accomplishments. For example, saying, "You only won that match because you got lucky," instead of acknowledging your hard work and skills.

Comparing to Others Negatively: Constantly comparing you unfavorably to others, implying you are inferior. For example, "Why can't you be more like Jenny? She's always successful."

Name-Calling: Being called demeaning names, which can chip away at your self-esteem.

"I hate you, bitch!" "Ugly whore!" "Filthy slut!" "Retard!" "Idiot!" "Asshole!" "Stupid loser!" etc.

Mockery: Making fun of your ambitions or appearance, dimin- ishing your self-worth.

"As if you could ever be an actress! You're not talented or pretty enough!"

"You're not good enough, you'll never achieve that!" "Ooh, you're trying to look special/pretty/sophisticated! You'll never be more than a 6/10!"

Mockery comes in so many forms, from verbal to physical cues.

Rolling eyes, smirking, or using dismissive gestures to undermine or ridicule your ideas or contributions can hurt just as much as nasty words.

Constant Monitoring: "Where Are You?"

Ever feel like you're in a reality show with your partner as the audience? Constant questions like "Where are you?" "Who are you with?" "What are you doing?" – it's not cute; it's controlling. It's like they need to keep tabs on you 24/7, which is super suffocating.

Invasion of Privacy: No Space to Breathe

Okay, so everyone needs their privacy, right? But if your partner's always snooping through your texts, emails, or social media, that's a major invasion of your personal space. Coercing you for pass- words, or worse, sneaking into your accounts – that's not love; that's breaking trust. And let's not even get started on not respecting your physical privacy. Major red flag!

Feeling that someone's jealous or invasive behavior is a sign of their love or care can be a common reaction, especially if you've been told that by your partner or read books which glamorize toxic relationships. However, jealousy and love are not the same. Love is about respecting the other person's autonomy and privacy, not controlling or monitoring them.

Gaslighting: Making you doubt your own memory and percep- tion, leaving you feeling confused and unstable.

Emotional Blackmail: Using threats or guilt to control your actions and decisions.

For instance, if your partner threatens to break up with you every time you disagree with them, you find yourself agreeing just to prevent the breakup. That's emotional black- mail, using threats to control you and manipulate your decisions.

Threats and Intimidation: Living in Fear

This one's scary. When your partner starts throwing threats around – like hurting themselves, you, or even leaking your private pics – it's a whole new level of not okay. It's super control- ling and can make you feel trapped.

Living under the cloud of these threats, you're always anxious, always scared. It's like you're tiptoeing around a sleeping beast, doing stuff just to keep the peace or prevent them from doing something drastic. And that fear? It's like a constant, heavy back- pack you can't take off.

Humiliation: Embarrassing you in public or in private, eroding your dignity. Exposing your secrets. Calling you humiliating names in public. For instance, Anna's boyfriend yelled at her in public. "Fucking whore, come here! Bitch, I'm waiting for you! Get your ugly, fat ass over here at once!" That was sooo hurtful and humiliating!

Other examples include saying something about you in public that you wished others didn't know. Something that makes you feel uncomfortable, ashamed, embarrassed, or unhappy.

Constant Criticism: Nothing you do seems right, leaving you feeling inadequate.

Manipulation: Okay, so picture this: You're at a party, and your BF or GF is like, "Hey, have a drink," but you're totally not feeling it. But they keep pushing, saying stuff like, "Don't be such a baby. Everyone else is doing it! I'll be embarrassed if you don't." And boom, you're sipping on something you didn't even want. That right there? That's manipulation. It's sneaky and way more than just peer pressure.

It's all about them wanting control, making you do things their way. It's not just drinks at parties; it could be anything – what you eat, drugs, hobbies, where you go, who you hang out with. And it's not cool because it's all about what they want, not what you're comfortable with.

The Guilt Game: Do you often feel guilty about your decisions or opinions in your relationship? Like, if you choose something different from what your partner wants, you're made to feel like the bad guy? That's manipulation, trying to control you by making you feel bad. You should be able to have your own opinions and make choices without feeling guilty about them.

Ever been in a situation where your partner's like, "If you really loved me, you'd do this," and suddenly, you're doing stuff you're not okay with? That's emotional blackmail. It's super manipulative and a total control move.

Imagine they start crying or saying they can't live without you unless you do what they want. It puts you in this weird spot where you feel guilty, even responsible for their feelings. It's like they're holding their emotions hostage, and the ransom to be paid? Your choices and freedom.

Guilt tripping is like a heavy backpack. The more you carry it, the more it weighs you down. It's when someone makes you feel guilty for not doing what they want.

Picture this: your cousin asks you to help him with his homework. You decline because you've planned a day out with your friends. He makes you feel guilty, saying you're letting him down and he's going to fail because of you (totally not true, folks!). That's guilt tripping – manipulating with guilt to get what they want.

I don't care about you: Respect is huge in any relationship. But if your partner disregards what you want, like, or even dream about, that's not just disrespectful; it's hurtful. When someone keeps forgetting or ignoring what matters to you, it can make you feel invisible, like you're not important. Habitually ignoring or speaking over you signals that your thoughts or opinions are unimportant. And that's not okay. Your opinions and dreams matter – don't let anyone make you think otherwise.

When Your Feelings Don't Count: Dismissing your feelings or thoughts as unimportant or wrong. "I don't care what you think! Your thoughts don't matter, they're stupid. Who cares what you have to say about that topic? You're stupid and you don't know anything about it!"

It's super frustrating when someone just brushes off how you feel or what you think. Invalidation can be like a silent killer in rela- tionships. If your partner's always dismissing your feelings or experiences, it can make you question your own reality. Your feelings are real and valid, and a good partner will recognize and respect that.

Withholding Affection: Using love and affection as a tool to manipulate and control.

For instance, your girlfriend might say "If you don't buy me that dress, I won't sleep with you."

Or "If you really love me, you'd paint your hair." And when you don't, they ignore you, ghost you, don't talk to you, and refuse to give you any affection.

Ignoring you: Stonewalling, silent treatment, blocking, ghosting, going cold, not talking to you because you didn't do what they wanted. That's not about being "hurt" by your actions, that's plain manipulation.

Isolation Tactics: Cutting you off from friends and family, making you feel alone and dependent. Forbidding you to see your friends. Making you feel guilty if you want to spend time with anyone other than your boyfriend/girlfriend. Treating it like a betrayal if you want to meet your friends or family.

Exclusion: Exclusion is a silent form of bullying. It's when your friends or significant other deliberately leave you out, isolate you, make you feel like you're not part of the group. They cold- shoulder you, don't invite you to their parties or events.

For instance, if your friends made plans without you. You find out about it on social media, a punch to the gut. You feel left out, you feel alone. That's exclusion. It's painful, it's isolating, and it's a sign of a toxic relationship.

When Flirting Crosses the Line: Trust on the Edge

Ever feel like your partner's a bit too friendly with others, and it's kinda not cool? Like, they're always chatting up other peeps, admiring other people's bodies and pictures, maybe even in a way that's a bit too much. They might talk about others in a sexual way that makes you feel super uncomfortable, or worse, compare you to them.

And then there's the sneaky stuff, like going out with someone else, sexting others, not telling you where they are if you ask, or spending the night somewhere and you're left wondering. Plus, their social media? Full of likes and thirsty comments on photos of hot girls or guys that make you feel uneasy. That's not just being friendly; it's breaking trust and totally disregarding your feelings.

It's tough, but knowing these signs helps you understand what's not okay in a relationship. Remember, you deserve someone who respects you, trusts you, and puts you in the spotlight because you're amazing just as you are.

Betrayal: Betrayal is like a knife in the back. It cuts deep, it hurts, and it leaves a wound that takes time to heal. It's when a friend or partner breaks your trust or lets you down when you needed them the most.

You trusted them, you confided in them, but they betrayed you. They revealed your deepest secret or exposed something private about you. It felt like a deep stab in your heart, worse than you thought it could. That's betrayal. It's a clear sign of a toxic relation- ship or friendship.

The "You Owe Me" Trap: Ever feel like your partner's keeping score? Like every nice thing they do comes with a price tag? They might say stuff like, "After all I've done for you, you can't even do this for me?" It's like they're running a tab, and you're always in debt. That's not love; that's making you feel obligated, and it's a sneaky way to control you. Love isn't about keeping score; it's about giving freely, without expecting something in return.

You deserve someone who respects you, trusts you, and loves you without making you feel obligated or trapped. It's about finding balance, not living in fear and dread.

"You're My Only Choice" Lie:

This one's rough. If your partner's telling you things like, "No one else will ever love you," or putting you down, calling you names, telling you you're a 6/10 and lucky to have them, or trying to make you think they're your only option, it's a cruel way to make you feel trapped, like you can't do any better.

But here's the truth: you are lovable, and there are people out there who will see your true worth. Don't let anyone make you feel less than amazing.

Reputation Games: The Dangerous Gossip

Okay, this one's serious. If your partner's spreading rumors about you or threatening to spill your secrets, that's way out of line. It's like they're holding your reputation hostage, using it to control you. And the thought of them sharing private photos? That's not just mean; it's a betrayal on a whole different level. This kind of behavior is about power, not love, and it can leave you feeling scared and trapped.

Dealing with a Narcissist: It's All About Them

Narcissism in a relationship is like a one-person show, and guess what? You're not the star. They've got this huge ego, always needing attention and admiration. They might put you down or brush off your feelings just to keep the spotlight on them.

Being with someone who's all about themselves can make you feel small, like your feelings don't matter. It's a cycle of them pulling the strings, and you're just there to applaud. But here's the thing: You're not a background character; you're the hero of your own story. Recognizing this behavior is key to stepping out of their show and into your own.

Always trust your feelings and know that you have the right to a relationship that makes you feel respected and loved. You got this, and there's a whole world of real, healthy love waiting for you. Stay strong and true to yourself!

Victim Blaming: Making you feel like everything's your fault, even their abusive actions.

"You made me do it! It's your fault I'm angry!"

Screaming: The Sound of Control: Yelling, shouting, and using nasty tones – it's like they're trying to control you with the volume of their voice. It's super intimidating and can make you feel small, scared, and like you can't speak up. That's not communication; that's just trying to win by being the loudest in the room. In a healthy relationship, problems are talked out, not yelled out.

Unhealthy Dependence: More Than Just Neediness:

Feeling like you're the only thing keeping your partner happy? That's a ton of pressure. They might make you feel like they're lost without you. But here's the thing: you're not responsible for fixing them or for being their only source of happiness. In a healthy rela- tionship, it's about supporting each other, not being someone's emotional lifeline. You're a partner, not a therapist. Remember, it's okay to take care of yourself too.

Keeping It Real: Recognizing Unhealthy Control

These tactics – manipulation, emotional blackmail, threats – they're all about taking away your power, making you feel small. Remember, in a good relationship, you feel free to be you, to make your own choices without fear or guilt.

If you find yourself facing this stuff, it's a sign to step back and think, "Is this really what I want?" Because, trust me, you deserve so much better. A relationship should lift you up, not bring you down.

Stay true to yourself, trust your gut, and never be afraid to reach out for help. You're stronger than you think, and you deserve to be happy, respected, and in control of your life. You got this!

Finding Your Voice and Your Power

In a healthy relationship, you get to be you – with all your choices, feelings, and dreams intact. If your partner's making you feel like you're losing parts of yourself, it's time to take a step back. Remember, you're awesome just as you are, and you deserve someone who celebrates that, not someone who tries to change it.

Always trust your instincts and remember, your feelings and thoughts are important. You deserve a relationship where you feel heard, seen, and respected. You got this, and you're not alone!

THE TOLL ON YOUR HEART AND MIND

Emotional abuse isn't just about bad feelings; it's damaging on a deeper level:

- **Self-Esteem**: It can leave you feeling worthless, doubting your own value.
- **Mental Health**: You might feel constantly anxious, depressed, or even scared.
- **Confidence**: Constant belittling can make you lose trust in yourself and your abilities.
- **Hope and Future**: You start to believe there's nothing better for you, trapping you in the cycle of abuse.

Recognizing the Unhealthy Patterns

Understanding these signs is the first step in acknowledging you might be in a toxic relationship. It's tough to admit, but it's crucial for your well-being.

Remember, emotional abuse is never okay. It's not about love; it's about control. You deserve to be treated with respect, to feel safe and loved for who you are.

Breaking Free

If you see these signs in your relationship, it's time to think about your next steps. Reach out for support, whether it's friends, family, or professionals. You're not alone, and you deserve a healthy, happy relationship where you can thrive.

Remember, your feelings are valid, your experiences are real, and you have the right to a relationship free from emotional abuse. You got this, and there's a whole world of respect and love waiting for you.

AM I BEING EMOTIONALLY ABUSED?

Sometimes, it's hard to see emotional abuse, especially when it's wrapped up in 'love.' But if these lines sound familiar, it might be time to take a closer look:

Typical Things Abusers Say:

"No one else will love you like I do."

"It's your fault that I have to keep an eye on you."

"I don't want you hanging out with those friends anymore." "You're crazy – I never said any of that."

"Nobody else needs to know anything about our relationship."

"Why can't you be more like [someone else]?" "You're lucky I put up with you."

"You're [ugly, stupid, fat, unworthy, etc.]."

"You're not [good, smart, pretty, cool, sexy, etc.] enough."

What It Feels Like

Emotional abuse can stir up a bunch of heavy feelings. Check if any of these ring a bell:

- Constantly worried you'll do something wrong that will upset your partner.

- Feeling pressured to always be available and respond instantly to messages.
- Guilt-tripping for spending time away from your partner.
- Feeling like you and your partner are in a world of your own, isolated from others.
- Being put down by your partner's words or actions.
- Doubting your own memory and reality because of their denials and lies.

How Emotional Abuse Harms You

Emotional abuse isn't just a bunch of bad feelings – it can do real, lasting damage:

1. **Self-Image and Self-Esteem**: You start believing you're not good, smart, or pretty enough. It's like they're rewriting your self-view.
2. **Self-Worth**: You might start feeling like you deserve this treatment, that you don't deserve better. But that's just the abuse talking.
3. **Mental Health**: Constant unhappiness, anxiety, stress, and fear become your norm. It's like living under a dark cloud.
4. **Shame & Guilt**: You blame yourself, feeling guilty and ashamed, even though you're the victim.
5. **Hope & Future**: Your outlook on life gets bleak. You start thinking this is all there is for you, but that's not true.

Recognizing Emotional Abuse

If these signs and feelings sound familiar, it might be time to take a step back and think about your relationship. Emotional abuse is sneaky, but recognizing it is the first step towards healing.

Remember, you deserve to be treated with love, respect, and kind- ness – not fear, control, or belittlement. Your worth isn't defined by someone else's treatment of you. You are valuable, lovable, and deserving of a happy, healthy rela- tionship.

Don't be afraid to reach out for support, whether it's friends, family, or professional help. You're not alone in this, and there's a brighter, happier path ahead. You got this!

3

GASLIGHTING

Imagine you're in a maze, and every time you think you've found the way out, the walls shift. That's what gaslighting feels like. It's when someone makes you question your reality, your

memory, your perceptions. What exactly is Gaslighting?!

It's like this mind game some people play in relationships to make you question your own reality. Think of it as a way of controlling you by making you doubt your own thoughts, feelings, and experi- ences. They do it to get away with their wrong behavior or to make you depend on them. It's sneaky, it's harmful, and it's totally not okay.

Gaslighting can make you feel like you're crazy even when you're perfectly sane.

Common Signs of Gaslighting

Twisting the Truth: If your partner's always twisting your words or the truth, making you feel like you're going crazy, that's gaslighting.

Downplaying what they did: If you complain about what they said or did, they might make you feel ashamed or silly by saying stuff like "You're too sensitive," "You're overacting," or "You should hear yourself, you sound crazy!"

Denying Stuff They Did: You saw them do something or heard them say something, but they flat-out deny it ever happened. "I never said that! You're imagining things!" "I never hit you, you're crazy! You need help!" It could be something smaller, like your friend borrowing your favorite hoodie and losing it. When you confront them, they insist they never borrowed it. You start doubting your

memory, even though you clearly remember lending it to them. That's gaslighting – making you question your own reality.

- **Constantly Questioning Your Memory:** They keep saying things like, "You're remembering it wrong," or "You're so forgetful."
- **Making You Doubt Your Sanity:** They might even say things like, "You're being paranoid." "That isn't

FROM PAIN TO EMPOWERMENT: | 69

what happened, can't you remember?" "You have serious problems."

The Origin Story of 'Gaslighting'

Ever wondered where the term 'gaslighting' came from? Flashback to 1944, there's this movie called 'Gaslight.' In it, this dude manip- ulates his wife big time, making her think she's losing her mind. It's all about him messing with her reality – turning lights down low, then denying it's happening, all to make her doubt her sanity. Creepy, right? That's where we get the term 'gaslighting.'

Gaslighting IRL: How It Plays Out

Fast forward to today, and gaslighting's not just in old movies; it's happening in real relationships. It's like this mind trick where someone makes you question your own memories and sanity.

Picture this: Your boyfriend says something super hurtful, but when you bring it up later, he's like, "I never said that. Are you making stuff up again?" Or worse, imagine he gets physically aggressive, but the next day, he totally denies it and even acts offended that you'd accuse him. He's like, "Me? Hit you? You must be going crazy, because I would never do something like that."

It's this twisted way of flipping the script, making you the problem when you're really the victim. It's like living in a funhouse mirror where nothing looks or feels right.

Getting the lowdown on gaslighting is key because it helps you spot these mind games before they mess with your head too much. Knowing what it looks like – the denial, the twisting of truth, the making you doubt yourself – that's your shield. It helps you see the situation for what it is: manipulation, not your imagination.

So, that's the deal with gaslighting. It's tricky, it's harmful, but knowing about it gives you the power to say, "Nah, I see what you're doing, and I'm not playing this game." Stay aware, stay true to yourself, and remember, your reality is yours, no one else's.

Am I Being Gaslit?

Answer these 7 questions...

If you're feeling a bit lost and wondering if you're being gaslit, here are some questions to ask yourself:

1. Do I find myself constantly second-guessing my memory?
2. Am I always apologizing, even when I don't think I did anything wrong?
3. Do I feel more anxious and less confident than I used to be?
4. Am I often told that I'm too sensitive or overreacting?
5. Do I feel isolated or cut off from friends and family?

6. Am I starting to believe I'm the problem in the relationship?

7. Do I feel like I can't do anything right in my partner's eyes?

Gaslighting is like this invisible chain that can hold you back and make you feel trapped in your own mind. If these questions are hitting home, it might be time to take a step back and assess your relationship.

Remember, your feelings and memories are valid, and no one has the right to make you doubt your truth.

GASLIGHTING STORIES

The Blame Game

Susie: "I remember when Mike got super mad over a text I didn't even send. He accused me of talking to other guys. When I showed him my phone to prove I didn't, he flipped it, saying, "You always make me out to be the bad guy." Suddenly, I was apologizing for his jealousy. It was messed up."

Unhealthy Behavior (Red Flags):

Mike's baseless accusations and then flipping the situation to make himself the victim is classic gaslighting. It's super unhealthy because it makes Susie feel like she's in the wrong, even when she's not.

Making someone apologize for your own jealousy? That's a manipulation tactic. It's turning the tables to avoid responsibility.

Healthy Behavior (Green Flags):

In a healthy relationship, trust is key. If Mike had concerns, he should've calmly discussed them, not thrown accusations.

A good partner takes responsibility for their feelings. They don't blame you for their emotions.

The Denial Trick

Michelle: "So, there was this time I caught Jake liking and commenting on his ex's pics on Insta. He commented really loving stuff, the same things he said to me when we met. When I asked him about it, he straight-up denied it. He even said, 'That's not my account.' He told me I was being overly jealous. The next day all the comments he'd posted were gone and when I asked why he'd deleted them, he laughed and said 'You're crazy! You imagined it!' I started questioning if I was seeing things and wondering if I was crazy."

Unhealthy Behavior (Red Flags):

Jake's denial and then accusing Michelle of being jealous is a serious red flag. It's a way of making her doubt what she clearly saw.

Deleting the comments and then claiming they never

existed? That's gaslighting 101. It's trying to mess with your perception of reality.

Healthy Behavior (Green Flags):

Transparency is crucial in relationships. If Jake was upfront about his interactions, there would be no need for denials or cover-ups.

A supportive partner would address your concerns, not dismiss them or make you feel 'crazy.'

Gaslighting is all about control and creating doubt in your mind. It's important to trust your gut and remember, you're not 'crazy.' If you feel like something's off, it probably is.

Remember, healthy relationships are built on trust, honesty, and mutual respect, not confusion and manipulation. You deserve someone who treats you with kindness and understanding, not someone who plays mind games.

The "You're Too Sensitive" Line

Bruce: *"Every time I got upset about something Leo said, he'd roll his eyes and go, 'You're too sensitive.' Like when he joked about my weight. It made me feel like my feelings weren't valid, that I was just overreacting. But I wasn't, right?"*

Unhealthy Behavior (Red Flags):

Leo dismissing your feelings with a "You're too sensitive" is not cool. It's a way to invalidate your emotions and make you doubt yourself.

Making jokes about sensitive topics like weight and then calling you sensitive for getting upset is manipulative. It's like he's trying to make it your fault for reacting.

Healthy Behavior (Green Flags):

In a healthy relationship, your partner respects your feelings. If something upsets you, they listen and understand, not dismiss.

A caring partner is mindful of their words and apologizes if they hurt you, instead of making you feel like you're over-reacting.

This type of behavior shows classic signs of emotional manipula- tion. It's important to recognize that your feelings are valid and you're not overreacting. In healthy relation-ships, there's mutual respect and understanding, not guilt-tripping and invalidation.

Remember, you have the right to feel respected and heard in your relationship. If you're constantly feeling invalidated or guilty, it might be time to reevaluate the dynamics of your relationship. You deserve to be treated with kindness and respect, always.

The Guilt Trip

Chris: *"Emma had this way of making everything my fault. If she was upset, somehow it was because of something I did or didn't do. If I bought her flowers, she'd get angry saying I was ruining the planet, and when I didn't buy them, she'd get angry too, saying I* *didn't love her. When I offered to get a pizza she snapped she hated pizza, but then the next time she was angry I didn't order pizza and said she loves it and that I'm selfish and unloving and never remember what she likes. I felt like I was always tiptoeing around her, trying to please her, trying not to upset her. It was exhausting, always feeling guilty like I did something wrong."*

Unhealthy Behavior (Red Flags):

Emma's constant shifting of blame and making contradictory demands is a classic guilt trip. It's designed to keep you confused and feeling at fault.

Getting mad no matter what you do, like the flowers and pizza situations, is about control, not about the actions themselves. It's a way to keep you off-balance.

Healthy Behavior (Green Flags):

In a good relationship, communication is clear and consistent. Your partner doesn't flip-flop on their preferences just to make you feel guilty.

A supportive partner appreciates your efforts and doesn't use them as an opportunity to guilt-trip or control you.

The Gaslighting Guru

"This one time, I overheard Alex talking trash about me to his friends. When I confronted him, he laughed and said, 'You're hearing things. I said nothing like that.' I started doubting my own ears. When I insisted, he looked so hurt and said, 'How could you?

You hurt me so much! Why are you inventing these lies? What are you trying to do to me?' It was like he had this power to twist reality. I apologized and then later I felt really angry and upset."

Unhealthy Behavior (Red Flags):

Alex denying he said anything and then acting hurt is classic gaslighting. He's making you question your own reality and then flipping it to make you the bad guy.

Him twisting the situation to make you apologize, even though he was in the wrong, is a manipulative power play. It's all about controlling the narrative.

Healthy Behavior (Green Flags):

In a healthy relationship, if there's a misunderstanding or disagreement, both people talk it out respectfully. They don't deny or twist what happened.

A caring partner doesn't make you doubt your own senses or memories. They value honesty and clear communication.

The Love Bomber

"At first, Dylan was all sweet and romantic. He'd shower me with compliments and gifts. But when I wanted to spend time with my friends, he'd get upset and say, 'You don't love me like I love you.' He made me feel guilty for having a life outside of him. I ended up losing all my friends, hardly spending time with my family, and being completely dependent on him. It took me a while to see it was manipulation."

Unhealthy Behavior (Red Flags):

Dylan's over-the-top affection turning into guilt trips when you do your own thing is a form of love bombing. It's about over- whelming you with love and then using it as leverage.

Making you feel guilty for spending time with others and leading you to become isolated from friends and family is a control tactic. It's about making you dependent on him.

Healthy Behavior (Green Flags):

A healthy partner encourages independence and respects your need for space and other relationships. They support your friend- ships and family ties.

Love in a healthy relationship doesn't come with conditions or strings attached. It's freely given and doesn't change based on what you do.

Gaslighting and love bombing can leave you feeling confused, isolated, and dependent. It's important to recognize these tactics for what they are and understand that they're not signs of a healthy relationship.

Remember, you deserve to be in a relationship where you feel safe, respected, and free to be yourself. Your thoughts, feelings, and independence are important. Trust yourself, and don't be afraid to seek support if you find yourself in a situation like this. You're stronger than you think, and you deserve real, honest love.

That wraps up our look at gaslighting. It's a tough topic, but understanding it is super important in recognizing and dealing with toxic relationships. Up next, we'll explore how to reclaim your voice and trust in yourself again. Stay strong, and remember, you're not alone in this journey.

4

WHEN WORDS STING

DEALING WITH INSULTS IN YOUR RELATIONSHIP

Hey there!

So, we're going to chat about something kinda tough but super important – dealing with insults in rela- tionships. Ever been in a spot where someone you totally care about throws a hurtful comment your way? Yeah, it's rough. And hey, it's totally okay to feel upset about it. We're all about keeping it real here, and some- times, 'real' means tackling the tough stuff.

So, let's get into it, together.

From Your Boo: The 'Just Kidding' Jabs: Imagine this: You're hanging out with your SO, and you're all excited about this idea you have. But as soon as you share it, they're like, "That's kinda dumb, don't you think?" or "Jane's ideas always suck!" and then hit you with a "Just kidding!"

It stings, right? It's like they're putting you down but trying to play it off as a joke.

Bae's Body Comments: You're trying on outfits for a night out, and your bae goes, "Hmm, have you put on weight?" Ouch.

It's one thing to have a healthy chat about fitness or health, but it's a whole other thing to feel judged about your body by someone who's supposed to have your back.

'Friendly' Fire: Ever had a friend who drops a nasty comment, then follows it with a LOL or a poo emoji? Like, you post a selfie and they're like, "You look like

today, haha!" Not cool. Friends should lift you up, not bring you down, even if they say it's just a joke.

Friendship Fails: This one's tough. Say your bestie sees your report card and goes, "Another D? Wow, you're a real failure." That hits deep, right? Friends should be your cheer squad, not your critique panel.

No respect: It starts small, so small you don't pay much attention at first. You're chilling with your bae, and suddenly, out of nowhere, they drop a mean joke about your outfit. You laugh it off, but deep down, it hurts.

Next thing you know, these 'jokes' become a regular thing. They're calling you names, dissing your interests, mocking you... It's like, where's the respect, right?

Okay, let's get real. When someone you're into starts throwing insults, it's not just 'teasing.' It's straight-up toxic.

It's not about being too sensitive; it's about being respected.

When they diss you, it's like they're chipping away at your self- esteem. And that's never okay. Your feelings? Totally valid.

Picture this: You share a goofy pic of yourself in PJs. A healthy response? Your partner's like, 'OMG, you're adorable ' or 'That's so you, LOL.'

They lift you up, not tear you down. That's respect. That's love.

An unhealthy reaction would be calling you lumpy, fat, dorky, or even a fugly bitch.

If you put on weight, a caring friend might invite you to go jogging with her or play tennis together. A toxic friend might tell you to buy a bigger dress and maybe even say it with a gloating smile, secretly happy that you're putting on weight.

Worst of all, when you let someone insult you once, they

never stop. It's like they realize you'll swallow it, so they gleefully keep on giving you more.

"So at first it was like they were just teasing, ya know? But then, it got kinda mean. Like, suddenly everything I do is not cool enough for them. My clothes, the food I eat, the peeps I hang out with, the tunes I'm into, even the shows I binge-watch – it's like everything's up for their critique. Seriously, what's up with that?"

— CHRISTINE

Insults can come in many forms. They're those nasty comments about your look, style, ideas, brains, abilities, even your dreams. In a toxic relationship, insults aren't just random words; they're like weapons used to tear you down, control you, and make you feel small.

Why do they do it? It's not because those things are true; it's to chip away at your self-esteem. They want to make you feel like you're nothing without them, so you'll stick around and put up with their trash talk.

Sometimes, we find it hard to separate what's an insult from what's the truth. Some people will even deny having been insulted, saying, "What? That was an insult? But I thought it was true!" So let's take a quick look at what are some totally not okay ways of speaking to you (or to anyone):

Insults Decoded

1. Anything that highlights something that's bad or wrong about you.

- This includes pointing out a big nose, big ears, crooked legs, weight, accent, hair, skin, or anything else. Real, kind, loving friends (and of course a BF/GF) don't do this. They don't pick on your faults or highlight them. They look for nice things about you and highlight those. Yeah, maybe someone's got acne, and sure, it's not pretty, but pointing it out is not a kind thing to do. That's mean and hurtful.

2. Anything that makes you feel ashamed, sad, scared, or bad for being who you are.

- If they tell you that being you is wrong, that you're stupid, that what you like is bad, that you shouldn't have those dreams and goals... all that is toxic. It's completely okay for you to be unique, to be yourself, to be different. You don't have to be a clone of anyone or to change who you are to fit their requirements.

THE IMPACT OF INSULTS ON SELF-PERCEPTION

Alright, let's get real for a sec. When someone's constantly throwing shade your way, it can seriously mess with how you see yourself. You might start thinking, "Maybe I am not smart enough," or "Am I really that unattractive?" It's like their words start to echo in your mind, and that's tough.

Here's why this is super harmful: you start believing these insults. You might feel super insecure at a party, thinking everyone's judging you. Or maybe you start hating on your own body, which is totally not okay. These negative vibes can stop you from trying new stuff because you're scared of messing up and hearing those harsh words again. It's a cycle of feeling down, and that's not what you deserve.

CLARIFYING WHAT'S NOT OKAY

First off, let's make one thing crystal clear: insults, in any form, are NOT okay. Period.

It's not about you 'not taking a joke' or being 'too sensitive.' It's about respect, and insults have zero place in any healthy relationship.

Sometimes, people think that if you care about someone, you should put up with their bad behavior. Sometimes they'll tell you they're insulting you because they *care about you* and want to help you improve or something like that. Nah, that's not how it works. Love is about lifting each other up, not tearing each other down.

If someone's insulting you, that's on them, not you. You're not the words they throw at you. You're way more than that.

And here's another important thing: even if there's some truth in their words (like maybe you did gain a little weight, or you got a D instead of an A), it's still not okay for them to use that against you. Getting a D may mean you failed that exam, but it doesn't define YOU as a failure! Being over- weight doesn't mean you're ugly, greedy, or anything else hurtful they say.

Constructive criticism is one thing, but insults? They're never a sign of love or care. They're toxic, and they hurt. And you don't have to stand for it.

Take Bruce and Emma, for example. Bruce is all about the put- downs, telling Emma her hair and clothes are whack, calling her stupid, and making her feel totally unlovable.

"No one else will ever love you! You're lucky to have me." Not cool, Bruce.

Emma starts to believe this trash talk, thinking she's lucky to have even him. But here's the truth bomb: Emma's amazing as she is. If she ditched Bruce, she could totally find someone who'd love her for her without wanting to change a single thing.

Remember: Insults Aren't About You

When someone throws insults your way, it's more about their own issues – their inner 'monsters,' not you. Being dissed about your looks, brains, or dreams is not only wrong, but it's also not your fault.

You deserve the good stuff – love, respect, and support. Being around people who make you feel great about being you? That's the goal. So remember, you're not the problem, and you totally deserve to be treated like the amazing person you are.

JAY'S STORY

Meet Jay. He's always been more into music and art than algebra. So when he scored a D on his math exam, it wasn't a huge shock. But what did shock him was his girlfriend's reaction: "A D? You loser! You're a failure! I'm ashamed to date you!"

Those words hit Jay like a ton of bricks. He started to see himself through his girlfriend's disappointed eyes. He'd hear 'idiot' and 'loser' echo in his head whenever he struggled with homework. It wasn't just math anymore; these labels started to seep into every part of his life. Jay began to believe he was destined to fail in everything he tried.

But here's the thing: one grade doesn't define who you are or what you're capable of. Just because Jay didn't ace math doesn't mean he's not smart or talented in a zillion other ways. And it definitely doesn't mean he's unlovable or doomed to fail forever.

Flipping the Script on Failure

So, how do we turn this around? First up, know this: Failure in one thing doesn't make you a failure in life.

Everybody messes up sometimes. It's part of being human. What matters is what you learn from it and how you bounce back.

Remember, you're not the labels people slap on you. You're way more than your latest grade or mistake. You've got whole galaxies of strengths and talents that one test can't even begin to measure.

Think about it: Maybe you're an amazing friend, a brilliant guitarist, or you've got a sense of humor that can light up a room. Those things count. Big time. And they say way more about you than a letter on a piece of paper.

And here's another key point: Just because you stumbled this time doesn't mean you're going to trip up every time. Life's full of chances to show what you're made of. So, maybe math isn't your jam – that's cool. You've got other jams where you totally rock.

So, next time you feel that weight of being called 'stupid' or a 'fail- ure,' take a step back. Breathe. Remind yourself of all the awesome stuff you do, all the people who get your jokes, who dig your music, who love you for being the real, amazing you.

EMILY'S STORY

Meet Emily. She's a bright, fun-loving girl, but yeah, she's a bit on the curvy side. Lately, her boyfriend's been dropping comments like, "Are you sure you want that extra slice of pizza? You're already getting fat." It started as a one-off, but now it's like his go- to joke.

At first, Emily laughed it off, but those words started to stick. She began skipping meals, feeling self-conscious every time she ate around him. She'd stand in front of her mirror, analyzing every curve, every bit of her she used to love. Parties? Forget them. She was convinced everyone was judging her, just like her boyfriend did.

What Emily didn't realize was how these insults were reshaping her view of herself. She went from this bubbly, confident girl to someone who shied away from the spot-light, afraid of being judged. It wasn't just about her body anymore; it started affecting her confidence in school, her willingness to speak up, her belief in her own worth.

Dismantling Negative Beliefs

Now, let's talk about flipping the script. Just like Emily, you might find yourself believing these negative things. But guess what? They're not your truth. They're someone else's unfair judgments.

It's time to start challenging those beliefs. Ask yourself, "Why should someone else's opinion define me?" You're the one who gets to decide who you are, not them. Remember, you're awesome in a million ways they might never see, and that's their loss.

When these negative thoughts creep in, hit pause. Remind yourself of your achievements, your talents, your dreams – the stuff that makes you, you. It's like building an invisible shield around your- self, made of all the good stuff, keeping the bad stuff out.

THE TRUTH ABOUT INSULTS AND LOVE

Fam, let's get something straight: love and insults are like oil and water – they just don't mix.

In a healthy relationship, it's all about respect and lifting each other up. Think about it like being each other's cheer-leaders. You celebrate the wins, support through the losses, and always have each other's backs.

But if someone's dissing you, making fun of your dreams, or throwing shade on your choices, that's not cool. That's the oppo- site of what love's about. Love should make you feel like you're on top of the world, not like you're constantly trying to dig yourself out of a hole.

Love is Lifting, Not Lowering

Remember, someone who really cares about you will respect you – your thoughts, feelings, and, yeah, even your quirks. They won't try to bring you down or make you feel small.

Love's about building something awesome together, not tearing each other apart.

HEALTHY RELATIONSHIPS

Flip the script to a healthy relationship, and it's a whole different vibe. It's all about building each other up, not tearing each other down.

Encouragement Over Criticism: They're your cheerleader, celebrating your wins and supporting your dreams.

Loving the Real You: They dig you just as you are. No 'fixer-upper' projects here – just pure, 'you're awesome' vibes.

No Room for Mockery: They don't make fun of your looks, smarts, or hopes. That's just not how they roll.

5

MANIPULATION

The Sneaky Side of Teen Relationships

Hey there! So, we're diving into some pretty intense stuff in this part of our journey – manipulation and control in teen relationships. It's like we're opening the lid on a box of tricks some peeps use to get their way, and trust me, it's not all sunshine and rainbows.

What's Manipulation, Anyway?

Manipulation is like a game of chess, but with emotions. It's when someone tries to influence your actions or feelings, but not in a good way. They're not upfront about it; they're sneaky, pulling strings behind the scenes to make you do what they want.

Why Do Some Peeps Manipulate?

You might wonder, "Why would someone do that?" Well, sometimes, people manipulate because they want to feel in control. It's like they're not confident enough to deal with things straight up, so they twist and turn situations to their advantage.

And get this, there are all sorts of manipulation tactics out there:

- **False Truths:** Twisting words to make you feel bad about yourself, give up what you want, agree to do what they want, or even make you believe you're unworthy or stupid.
- **The Guilt Trip**: Making you feel guilty to get their way.
- **Gaslighting**: Making you doubt your own memory or feelings.
- **Love Bombing**: Overwhelming you with affection to make you dependent.
- **Playing the Victim**: Acting like they're the hurt one to gain sympathy.

The real kicker? Often, what the manipulator wants isn't what's best for you. It's about their needs, their desires, not yours. They might convince you to ditch your friends, change how you dress, or even give up on your dreams – all to keep you under their thumb.

The Control Factor

And then there's control. It's like manipulation's cousin. It's when someone wants to dictate every part of your life – who you hang out with, where you go, even what you think. It's all about keeping you on a leash, so they feel powerful.

So, as we go through this section, keep your eyes open and your mind sharp. Understanding these tricks can help you spot them in real life and keep you from falling into those traps. Remember, you deserve to be in a relationship where you're respected, valued, and free to be yourself – not controlled or manipulated.

Let's gear up to unravel these tactics and learn how to stand strong against them. You've got this, and remember, knowledge is your superpower in the world of relationships. Let's dive in!

UNRAVELING THE DANGEROUS WEB OF 'FALSE TRUTHS'

Ever notice how sometimes, a small bit of truth gets twisted into a big, hurtful lie? That's what we call 'false truths.' It's like someone takes one tiny thing and blows it up into a full-on attack on who you are.

How They Generalize and Hurt

The Ugly Hairdo Becomes "You're Ugly": Say you try a new hairdo, and someone doesn't like it. Instead of just dissing the hairstyle, they go all, "You look ugly." Bam! Suddenly, it's not about the hair; it's about you as a person. **One Lost Game Turns Into "You're a Loser"**: You lose a sports match, and someone's like, "You're such a loser." Ouch. It's not just the game you lost; now it feels like your whole identity is being called a 'loser.'

The Harmful Impact

These kinds of insults can really mess with your head. You start thinking, "Am I really a failure or ugly?" Your self-esteem takes a hit, and your confidence? Down the drain. It's like wearing glasses that make everything about you look bad.

Sometimes, in a relationship, one person tries to play this twisted game where they use 'false truths' to make you feel small. Let's talk about Derek and his GF as an example.

Derek's Story: The Eiffel Tower Trap

Derek's GF is like a walking trivia game. She knows all sorts of random facts, like how fast a llama can sprint or the number of stairs in the Eiffel Tower. Cool, right? But here's the catch: She uses this knowledge to put Derek down. When Derek can't answer her trivia questions, she's all, "You don't know how many stairs the Eiffel Tower has? You're a stupid idiot! You don't know anything!"

The Half-Truth Hook

See, she's hooking him with a half-truth. Yeah, Derek doesn't know some random fact, but does that make him stupid? Heck no! But because there's a tiny bit of truth in what she says (the part about not knowing the number of stairs), Derek starts to believe the whole thing, including the 'stupid idiot' part.

Breaking Down the 'False Truth' Technique

This is where we need to get our detective hats on and do some critical thinking. Just because one part of a statement is true doesn't make the whole thing true. It's like a sandwich with a slice of truth and a whole lot of nonsense.

Critical Thinking to the Rescue

So, here's how to break it down:

Acknowledge the Fact: "Okay, so I don't know the number of stairs. True."

Challenge the Insult: "But hey, not knowing that doesn't make me stupid. I know tons of other cool stuff!"

Remember, your intelligence isn't measured by trivia, not knowing something someone asks, or measuring yourself against others. It's about how you think, learn, and see the world. Not knowing one thing doesn't erase all the awesome stuff you do know.

Flipping the Script: Own Your Knowledge

The next time someone tries to pull a 'Derek's GF' on you, remem- ber: what you don't know doesn't define you. You're smart in your own way, and not knowing one thing doesn't change who you are.

By understanding the trick of 'false truths,' you can start to see when someone's trying to manipulate you with half-baked state- ments. Stick to your guns, and remember, your worth isn't a quiz score. You're way more than that. Stay sharp, stay you!

Beliefs Shaping Actions

Our beliefs drive what we do and how we react. When you start buying into these false truths, like thinking you're unworthy or not good enough, it can change the whole course of your life. You might hold back from going after what you want, feel like you don't deserve good stuff, or worse, believe you deserve the bad stuff.

The Example of Jenny

Take Jenny, for example. She failed an exam, and someone told her, "You're so stupid." Since being 'stupid' seemed like a 'logical' reason, she believed it. Now, she's scared to speak up, try new things, or chase her dreams. It's like one false belief put up a bunch of roadblocks in her life.

Abusers' Manipulative Tactics

Abusers are pros at this game. They use these false truths to make their victims feel small, unworthy, and at fault. It's a way to keep control. If you believe you're the problem, you're less likely to stand up for yourself or think you deserve better.

It's the main reason why people let their partner hurt them, insult them, hit them, and even sexually abuse them – because they think they deserve it!

The Danger of Accepting False Truths

These false truths, because they seem to make sense at first, can trap you in a cycle of negative thinking. You start accepting the abuse, blaming yourself, feeling guilty, and thinking you're not

worthy of anything better. It's like living in a world where every mirror shows a distorted version of you.

But here's the thing: Just because someone says it doesn't make it true. You're not what they say you are. You're way more than a failed test, a lost game, or a hairstyle. You're a whole person with a ton of worth, and no one's flawed opinion can change that.

Remember, you have the power to challenge these false truths. Don't let someone else's words dictate your worth. You're worthy, you're enough, and you definitely deserve a life filled with love and respect. Stay strong and trust in your own truth.

Examples

The "Always Wrong" Trap

Alex and Sam are chillin' together, and Sam's talking about her favorite band. Out of nowhere, Alex goes, "You got the song title wrong. You always get things wrong." Sam starts to feel like maybe she's not that smart after all.

Typical Sentence: "You're always messing up. Can't you get anything right?"

The "Never Good Enough" Game

Bella tries her best to look nice for her date with Jordan. But when she shows up, Jordan smirks, "You're wearing that? You never look as good as other girls." Bella's confidence starts to crumble, feeling she'll never be pretty enough.

Typical Sentence: "Why can't you look more like [insert name]? You never dress well."

The "Constant Comparison" Con

Every time Mike and his GF, Leah, hang out, she compares him to her ex, saying things like, "My ex would have known how to fix this. You're just clueless." Mike begins to doubt his abilities, feeling inferior.

Typical Sentence: "My ex was so much better at this than you. You just don't measure up."

The "Love With Conditions" Lie

Emma's BF, Tyler, often says, "If you really loved me, you'd do this for me." So, Emma bends over backward trying to prove her love, fearing that she's not loving enough as she is.

Typical Sentence: "If you really loved me, you wouldn't argue. You'd just do what I say."

The "Isolation Tactic" Twist

Whenever Hannah wants to hang with friends, her BF, Chris, guilts her, saying, "You'd rather be with them than me. Guess I'm not important." Hannah starts to feel guilty for having a life outside of him.

Typical Sentence: "You always choose others over me. I guess I'm just not that important to you."

Remember, these 'false truths' are nothing more than manipula- tion tactics. They're designed to make you doubt yourself and feel reliant on the abuser. It's important to recognize them for what they are – tools of control, not reflections of your true worth. You're way more than these twisted words. Stay aware and stay strong!

6

GUILT TRIP

WHAT'S A GUILT TRIP?

So, the guilt trip is like this emotional rollercoaster someone takes you on, except you never wanted the ticket. It's when someone tries to make you feel super guilty to get their way. They play on your emotions, making you feel bad so you'll do what they want.

Guilt trips come in different shades, but they all have the same goal: to make you feel like you owe them something or that you're in the wrong. Here are some classic moves:

1. The 'After Everything I've Done' Line

- **Story:** Jamie's BF always says, "After all I do for you, you can't spend Friday night with me?" Jamie starts feeling like she's ungrateful, even though she just wanted to hang with her friends.

- **Typical Sentence:** "I do so much for you, and you can't even do this one thing for me?"

2. The 'You Don't Care About Me' Accusation

- **Story:** Every time Alex wants to do something on his own, his GF drops, "You'd rather do that than be with me. You don't care about us." Alex ends up canceling his plans, feeling guilty for wanting some 'me' time.
- **Typical Sentence:** "If you really cared about me, you wouldn't go out with your friends tonight."

3. The 'I'm Always Last' Pity Party

- **Story:** When Emma chooses to study instead of texting back immediately, her BF sends, "Guess I'm just not that important to you. You always put me last." Emma feels like she's being a bad GF, even though she's just trying to ace her exams.
- **Typical Sentence:** "You always make me feel like I'm the last thing on your list."

4. Why Guilt Trips Are Super Uncool

- Guilt trips are like emotional handcuffs. They try to lock you into doing things out of guilt, not because you want to. It's a form of control that messes with your head and makes you second-guess your choices.

THE TRUTH ABOUT GUILT TRIPS

Remember, just because someone tries to make you feel guilty doesn't mean you've done anything wrong. You have the right to your own time, choices, and feelings. You deserve to be happy and do things that make you happy, even if it involves time without your partner. Don't let anyone's guilt trip detour your journey.

Embracing Your Uniqueness and Resisting Manipulation

Guilt trips can be tough to handle, but remember, you're in control of your own life. Your time, your space, your choices – they're yours, and they matter. Use these affirmations and journal prompts to help you stay strong, make decisions that are right for you, and resist manipulative tactics. You're not just a character in someone else's story; you're the author of your own.

Stay true to yourself, and remember, you're amazing just the way you are. Your journey is yours to shape, and you have the power to steer it in the direction that brings you joy and fulfillment. Keep shining, keep growing, and keep being you!

7

CONTROL

UNPACKING CONTROL IN RELATIONSHIPS

Hey, so let's talk about control – it's like when someone's trying to play director in the movie of your life. And not in a cool, artistic way, but in a way that makes you feel like you're losing your freedom.

The Many Faces of Control

Control can sneak into relationships in all kinds of sneaky ways. Here are a few you might recognize:

The Schedule Boss

- Lily's BF, Mark, always needs to know where she is, who she's with, and what she's doing – like, all the time. He even gets mad if she doesn't text back right away. It's like he's her personal scheduler, but without the chill.

- **Typical Sentence:** "Why didn't you text me back immediately? Where were you?"
- You don't have to 'report' on where you are, what you're doing, or whom you're talking to. That's not love, that's control.

The Opinion Overrider

- Whenever Tyler and his GF, Ava, are choosing a movie, Tyler's choice is somehow always 'wrong.' Ava insists on picking every time, saying Tyler's choice are terrible and she knows better what they'll both enjoy.
- **Typical Sentence:** "We're watching this; you always choose boring movies."
- Everyone has the right to their opinions. Being told your choices are bad, wrong, stupid, boring etc. is disrespectful and offensive. A loving partner cares about what you like and want.

Dream Crusher

- Mike shared his dream to be a lawyer. His GF laughed at him and said "You're not smart enough!

You'd never make it through law school! Don't be silly! You should be a truck driver instead."

- So not true. Remember, you can be anything you want to be! Telling you that your dreams are unattainable is hurtful, harmful, and wrong. If you want to be something, you can find a way to be it, no matter what anyone says.

Don't do that!

- Julie loves playing tennis, but her boyfriend Rudy told her he thinks tennis is a stupid hobby and doesn't want her to play it anymore. To please him, she stopped playing tennis.
- That's totally wrong! If you love doing a certain hobby or sport – you have the full right to do it! You have the right to be happy and do things you enjoy.

The Fashion Policeman

- Jess loves her quirky style, but her GF, Erin, always criticizes her outfits, saying they're not 'cool enough.' Erin even tries to pick out Jess's clothes for her, making Jess feel like she's losing her sense of style – and self.
- **Typical Sentence:** "You're not wearing that, are you? Here, wear this instead; it looks better."

- Being told what to wear is totally not cool. A loving partner respects you and lets you choose your own style.

MICROMANAGING: WHEN CONTROL GETS TOO CLOSE

And then there's micromanaging – it's control, but up close and personal. It's like someone's watching you with a magnifying glass, making sure every little thing you do fits their script.

Why It's Unhealthy

This level of control can make you feel like you're skating on thin ice, always worried about making a 'mistake.' It's exhausting and can make you lose touch with who you are and what you want.

Breaking Free from the Control Cycle

In a healthy relationship, it's about support, not supervision. You should feel free to make your own choices, whether it's about how you spend your time, what you wear, what you post on social media, what career you want, or what movie you watch on Friday night.

Taking Back the Reins

So, if you find yourself in a relationship where you're feeling more controlled than cared for, it's time to speak up. Your opinions, your style, your choices – they matter. You're not someone's project to manage; you're a partner to be respected.

You deserve to be in a relationship where you can be your true self, not someone else's version of you. Stay strong, stay you, and never forget: your life, your rules. You got this!

8

NARCISSISTIC ABUSE

UNDERSTANDING NARCISSISTIC BEHAVIOR: SEEING THROUGH THE MASK

Hey, so have you ever been around someone who, like, totally thinks they're the center of the universe? They're always craving likes and hearts as if they're the hottest TikTok star? Well, that's kinda what it's like dealing with someone who's got narcissistic behavior. Let's break it down and see what makes them tick.

Looking for Likes, 24/7: You know someone who's always fishing for compliments? Like, they do a simple thing and expect a parade? They're always seeking that spotlight, turning every chat or situation into their personal fan club meeting. That's their excessive need for admiration showing up.

Empathy? What's That? Ever talked to someone who just doesn't get how you feel? You could be telling them about your rough day, and they just don't care? It's like talking to a wall – all they care about is themselves. That total lack of getting you is their lack of empathy.

'I'm the Best' Vibes: Think about that one person who's always bragging, like they're the hero of every story. They talk big, act like they're above everyone, and just can't stop showing off. That's their grandiose sense of self-importance.

'Treat Me Like Royalty': Got a friend or someone who acts like the world owes them everything? Like they expect VIP treatment everywhere, even if it's just a trip to the mall? That's their sense of entitlement.

Using You for Their Gain: And what about that person who always seems to take more than they give? They use your kindness, spill your secrets, and twist things around for their benefit. They're like emotional vampires. That's their exploitative behavior.

Understanding these signs is like being a relationship detective. It might seem tricky, but once you get it, you start seeing the real person, not just their social media facade.

Remember, dealing with someone who's got these traits isn't easy, but their actions aren't a reflection of your worth. You're not just a character in their drama; you're the hero of your own awesome story. You've got the power to write your own script, set your own scenes, and choose who gets a starring role in your life. So keep your head up and your boundaries strong!

Narcissistic Abuse in Teen Relationships: A Hidden Trap

Narcissists come in many shapes and sizes. Some might be friends, others lovers.

Have you ever been with someone who seems super charming at first but then turns into a control freak? That's a classic sign of a narcissistic partner. In teen relationships, this can look like:

Constant Need for Attention: Like, they want you to be all about them, 24/7. If you're not giving them constant praise or attention, things go south pretty quickly.

Jealousy Overload: They might get super jealous if you spend time with friends or even family. It's like they want to be your entire world.

Putting You Down: They often put you down, especially in front of others. It's their way of keeping you feeling small while they feel big.

Mind Games: They can be super manipulative, making you doubt your own feelings or beliefs. It's like living in a constant state of confusion.

Isolation: They might try to cut you off from your friends, saying stuff like, "You don't need anyone but me."

The Impact of Narcissistic Abuse: Being with someone like this can really mess with your head. You might start feeling like you're not good enough, or like you're always walking beneath a huge, dark storm cloud that might explode at any moment. It can drain your confidence, make you feel super insecure, and even lead to anxiety or depression.

Moving Forward: Recognizing and Healing from Narcissistic Abuse

Understanding these behaviors is super important. If you find yourself in a relationship that feels more draining than uplifting, that's a big red flag. Remember, real love is about respect, under- standing, and mutual support, not control and manipulation.

If you think you're in a relationship with a narcissistic partner, it's really important to talk to someone you trust. Reach out to a friend, a family member, or even a counselor. It's about getting the support you need to step back into your power and find your happiness again.

You're so much more than someone's ego boost or emotional punching bag. You're awesome, and you deserve to be treated with love and respect. Remember, it's okay to walk away from some- thing that hurts you. Your well-being and happiness come first. Always.

Use positive affirmations to reaffirm your own worth, do fun things you love, and spend time with caring people to rebuild your self-esteem.

THE DIGITAL BATTLE NO ONE ASKED FOR

So, cyberbullying – it's like having a bully, but instead of the schoolyard, they're hiding behind a screen. It's this messed-

up behavior where someone uses social media, texts, or any digital platform to hurt, scare, or mess with someone else.

Think about it: mean comments on your Insta posts, creepy DMs that make you feel unsafe, or those totally not-okay pics shared without your permission. Or maybe it's being tagged in some unflattering meme or being added to a group chat just to see them dissing you. And let's not forget those nasty emoji comments – like that poo emoji on your selfie. Not cool.

This isn't just some online drama; it's serious stuff. Cyber-bullying can leave marks that you can't see – like feeling super down about yourself or even scared to go online. It's like every time you check your phone, there's this storm of hate and negativity just waiting for you.

It's more than just words on a screen. It's digital poison, messing with your head and your heart. Your self-esteem takes a hit, and your mental health? That takes a beating too.

Recognizing the Impact

Cyberbullying can make the online world feel like a mine-field. You're constantly on edge, wondering what's waiting for you in your notifications. It's a kind of harassment that follows you everywhere – home, school, anywhere you've got your phone or computer.

Remember, what happens online is real. The pain, the fear, the anxiety – it's all valid. And if you're going through this, know that it's not your fault. No one has the right to treat you like that, online or offline.

Finding Support and Speaking Up

If you're dealing with cyberbullying, it's super important to reach out for help. Talk to someone you trust – a friend, a family member, a teacher. And remember, it's okay to take a break from social media, to step away from the storm.

You deserve to feel safe and respected, both in the real world and online. Don't let anyone's digital hate dim your shine. You're way stronger than their words.

When we talk about physical abuse, it's like discussing a storm that hits where it's supposed to be safe – your personal relationships.

Physical abuse is any action someone does that causes pain, injury or trauma to you through bodily contact. It's not just about the visible bruises or scars; it's also about the fear and the feeling of being trapped in a cycle of hurt.

Let's shed light on what physical abuse really is, the forms it can take, and bust some common myths surrounding it.

WHAT IS PHYSICAL ABUSE?

Physical abuse can wear many masks, and understanding these can help you recognize it, whether it's happening to you or someone you know.

1. **Pushing, Shoving, Biting, Spitting, Slapping, Shaking, Punching, Scratching, Kicking, or Holding Down**: These acts are direct, physical attacks on a person's body. They're not just 'losing control' or 'accidents.' They are deliberate actions to hurt and control.

2. **Threatening Gestures**: Actions that don't necessarily make contact but are meant to intimidate or threaten, like raising a fist or moving aggressively, are also abusive.

3. **Throwing Things at You or Near You**: This creates an environment of fear and intimidation, even if you're not physically hurt.

4. **Breaking Your Property, Punching Holes in Walls**: This is about showing power, making you feel unsafe even in your own space.

5. **Interfering While Driving**: Actions like grabbing the steering wheel or hitting someone while they're driving can put lives at risk.

6. **Suffocation and Strangulation**: Blocking your airways, pressing on your face or neck – these are seriously dangerous and can be life-threatening.

7. **Grabbing Your Face to Force Eye Contact**: This is about control, forcing you to engage when you might feel unsafe or scared.

8. **Using or Threatening to Use a Weapon**: Any threat involving weapons is a serious form of physical abuse.

9. **Blocking Your Exit**: Not allowing someone to leave a room or space is a form of imprisonment and control.

UNDERSTANDING THE ROLE OF ABUSE

Physical abuse is about power and control. It's an abuser's way of telling you, "I have power over you." It can leave you feeling scared, helpless, and isolated. But it's crucial to remember – you're not powerless.

Common Misconceptions about Abuse

Myth: Physical abuse only happens in certain types of rela- tion- ships or to certain types of people.

Reality: Physical abuse knows no boundaries. It can happen to anyone, regardless of age, gender, socioeconomic status, or educa- tion level.

Myth: If there are no bruises or physical signs, it's not abuse.

Reality: Not all physical abuse leaves visible marks, but the damage is just as real.

Myth: Physical abuse is always obvious.

Reality: Sometimes, the signs are subtle – a partner who seems too controlling or quick to anger, for instance.

Physical abuse is a severe violation of your personal space and safety. It's not just about the physical pain; it's also about the emotional scars it leaves. Remember, it's not your fault, and you're not alone. There are people and resources ready to help and support you. The first step towards safety is recognizing the abuse and reaching out for help. You deserve to be treated with respect and to live without fear.

ABUSE STORIES

Jill's Story

Jill, a sophomore, felt special and important when she started dating Josh, an older, charismatic boy. However, charm soon turned into control. Josh's temper, initially part of his "bad-boy" appeal, became a source of fear. When Jill heard rumors that he was betraying her and tried to discuss it, Josh reacted angrily. He yelled at her, shook her by her shoulders, and made her feel guilty for daring to suspect him of betraying her.

At a school dance, he insulted her over her outfit choice and refused to take pictures with her. If she made plans to see her friends without asking him for permission first, he'd freak out and scream at her. Jill did everything he wanted just to avoid conflicts, losing her own identity in the process.

Jill had a childhood friend called Tom. They were just friends, but Josh wouldn't have her talk to anyone of the opposite gender. One day, Josh snatched her phone and went through the messages. When he discovered texts from Tom, he hurled Jill against a wall and began to strangle her. "I'm going to kill you and dump your body in the river!" he threatened, his eyes burning with hate and jealousy. He kept squeezing her till Jill almost passed out. Then he released her and stormed off.

The next day, he cried and apologized, saying he'd never do it again. "It was your fault! You made me so jealous!" he said, unfairly shifting the blame onto Jill.

"I love you so much! You made me crazy! I promise I won't do it again!"

Jill fell for his lies. She even stopped talking to her good friend Tom just so as not to make Josh jealous.

Josh pleaded with her to keep it a secret and swore it wouldn't happen again. Jill kept it to herself, hoping for the best, but unfor- tunately, the cycle repeated.

The next time Josh hurt her, he left deep bruises that took a week to heal.

Each time after hurting her, he'd cry and beg for forgiveness, and Jill would keep hoping that *this time* he'd really stop. But he didn't; it just got worse.

Eventually he even stopped apologizing and began yelling at her, telling her, "It's your fault!" He'd come up with a new excuse each time, such as, "It's your fault because you're a disgusting bitch! You're stupid! You're ugly! You asked too many questions! You answered back! You shouldn't have said that to me. You should haven't asked to see your friends. You shouldn't have gone to that party. You shouldn't have followed that influencer..."

Unhealthy/Abusive Behaviors (Red Flags)

1. **Temper and Jealousy**: Josh's anger and possessiveness are early red flags.
2. **Controlling Behavior**: Telling Jill what to wear and requiring her to ask his permission before making plans are signs of control, not love.
3. **Physical Abuse**: The choking incident is a severe and dangerous form of abuse.
4. **Emotional Manipulation**: Josh's apologies and promises not to repeat the behavior are manipulative tactics to keep Jill from leaving or seeking help.

What a Healthy Relationship Looks Like (Green Flags)

1. **Respectful Communication**: Partners feel safe to express concerns and feelings without fear of anger or retribution.
2. **Independence and Trust**: Each person in a relationship has the freedom to make personal decisions, spend time with friends, and have their own identity.
3. **Physical Safety**: A healthy relationship never includes physical harm or the threat of violence *for any reason.*
4. **Support and Equality**: Partners should encourage each other's growth and respect each other as equals.

Jill's story highlights the importance of recognizing early warning signs and understanding what a healthy relationship entails. It's vital to listen to your gut feeling. If something makes you uncom- fortable or scared, it's a sign of an unhealthy toxic relationship. Remember, physical abuse and emotional manipulation are never acceptable. Seeking help is a brave and important step towards healing.

Amber's Story

"I remember the first time it happened like it was yesterday. I'm Amber, and I was just a typical high schooler. I met him, let's call him Mike. He was charming and everything seemed perfect at first.

It was a sunny day, just outside my house. My parents were inside, and everything seemed normal. Then, out of nowhere, during an argument I can't even remember, Mike hit me. It was so sudden, a slap that seemed to echo through the entire street. I was stunned, speechless, just standing there trying to process it.

Mike's eyes, they changed, you know? They looked so cold, so harsh. I was just a bit over five feet, and he towered over me, intimidating me and waiting for me to react. All I could muster was a whispered, "You just slapped me." He didn't say a word. He just stood there, and then after what felt like an eternity, he left.

I went inside, locked myself in the bathroom, and just stared at my reflection. I was in shock. I didn't cry or anything. I just couldn't believe what had happened. Mike had always been sweet before, and now this? It didn't make sense.

The worst part? I started making excuses for him. Maybe he had a bad day, maybe it was something I said. I thought I loved him, and I didn't want to give up on 'us'. I told myself maybe it was a one-time thing. But it wasn't. Things got worse, and the scary part is, I started seeing it as normal.

Looking back, I wish I had seen the red flags sooner. A healthy rela- tion- ship shouldn't involve fear, intimidation, or physical harm. Real love is about respect, understanding, and care. It took me a while, but I finally found the courage to leave him. That decision was tough, but it was the best one I ever made. I learned that I deserve to be treated with kindness, not fear."

Amber's story is a heartbreaking example of how physical abuse can shatter one's sense of reality and self-worth. She thought her relationship with Mike was rooted in love, but it turned out to be a frightening experience of violence and manipulation.

Amber's initial shock and disbelief when Mike first hit her are, sadly, common reactions. Mike's action of slapping her was not just a physical assault but also a deep emotional betrayal. It was WRONG, wrong, wrong! And there was NO excuse for it!

He should NOT have hit her. That was a bad, abusive thing to do.

Amber's reaction is not uncommon in such situations, as victims often grapple with confusion, disbelief, and a desperate attempt to rationalize the abuser's behavior. Amber trying to excuse Josh's actions due to his past, or her own supposed mistakes, is a typical part of the complex emotional turmoil that victims of abuse often experience.

However, despite the normalization of abuse in her relation-ship and the many reasons she stayed – fear, shame, and a distorted sense of love – she eventually recognized the need to escape this destructive cycle. Her decision to leave the relationship marked a courageous step towards reclaiming her life, peace, happiness, and dreams.

In a healthy relationship, respect, care, and mutual under-standing are foundational. Abuse, whether physical or emotional, has no place. In a healthy relationship, there's mutual respect, open communication, and the ability to live freely without fear.

Amber's journey from a victim of abuse to a survivor taking control of her life is a powerful reminder that **no one deserves to be abused**. Everyone has the right to be treated with dignity and respect. There's strength within each person to break free from abuse and rebuild a life filled with hope, love, and purpose.

" IT' S YOUR FAULT I HURT YOU! YOU MADE ME DO IT!"

When They Say It's Your Fault – It's Not!

Ever played a game where you get blamed for stuff that's totally out of your control? Like another character shoots at you or you fall into a trap that the game developer made, and someone's like, "That's totally your fault! You deserved it!" Crazy, right? Well, that's exactly what happens in some relationships when it comes to reacting to stuff.

In an abusive relationship, your partner might hurt you and then say things like, "You made me do it!" or, "If only you hadn't said that, I wouldn't have gotten so mad."

You might feel it's unfair but feel guilty and ashamed anyway.

But here's the thing – *it's never your fault. No one deserves to be hurt, EVER.*

Why It's Not Your Fault:

1. **Choice and Control**: Remember, everyone has a choice in how they react. One person might react in a cool, calm way. Another might react violently. If someone chooses to hurt you, it's on them, not you. Just like in a game, if someone shoots at you, it's their decision, not your fault.

2. **Blame Game**: Abusers often play the blame game to control and manipulate you. It's their way of avoiding responsibility for their actions. It's like a magician using misdirection – they want you to look away from what's really happening.

3. **Understanding the Damage**: Being constantly blamed can mess with your head. It can make you doubt yourself and even believe you're the problem. But that's the abuser's voice in your head, not the truth. It's like wearing glasses with the wrong prescription – it distorts your view of reality.

The Psychology Behind It

1. **Gaslighting**: This is when someone tries to make you doubt your own experiences and perceptions. Imagine if someone kept changing the rules of a

game but insisted they were always the same.
Confusing, right?

2. **Self-Doubt**: Constant blame can lead to self-doubt.
   It's like if you kept losing in a game and started to
   think maybe you're just bad at it, even if the game
   was rigged against you.
3. **Fear and Control**: Abusers use blame to create fear
   and maintain control. It's their way of keeping you in
   the game, even when it's harming you.

Breaking Free from Blame

1. **Affirm Your Reality**: Keep a journal or talk to
   trusted friends about what's happening. It's like
   keeping a scorecard – it helps you see the game for
   what it really is.
2. **Seek Support**: Talk to someone who understands,
   like a counselor or a support group. It's like getting a
   guide for a really tough game.
3. **Affirmations**: Practice telling yourself the truth –
   that you're worthy, you're capable, and you don't
   deserve to be treated badly. It's like giving yourself a
   pep talk before a big game.
4. **Understand Your Worth**: Remember, you're
   valuable and deserving of respect. Just like in a game,
   you're the main character in your life – don't let
   someone else control your story.

CONCLUSION: YOUR STRENGTH AND YOUR FUTURE

Realizing and accepting that the abuse and the blame aren't your fault is like leveling up in understanding yourself. It takes strength, but you've got it. You have the power to step out of the horror game and into a new reality where you're respected, loved, and safe.

Remember, in the story of your life, you're the hero – and heroes deserve happy endings.

HEALING FROM PHYSICAL ABUSE

Acknowledging the Trauma

Okay, so let's get real here. Healing from physical abuse is like fixing a broken bike. You can't just pretend it's all fine and ride on. You gotta acknowledge the broken wheel, the torn saddle, the broken breaks. It's super important to recognize that what happened to you was not okay, and it's left a mark, both inside and out.

Think of it like this: You've been through a storm. It's okay to admit that you got hit hard. Recognizing the impact is like saying, "Yeah, that storm was brutal, but I'm still standing." It's the first step in healing and getting stronger.

Seeking Support

You know how in games, you sometimes need to team up with others to beat the boss level? Same thing here. After facing some- thing as heavy as physical abuse, it's crucial to gather your squad –

this means doctors, counselors, therapists, and people who genuinely care about you.

Reach out for medical help if you need it. Those physical scars need professional care. And don't forget about your mental health. Talking to a therapist or counselor is like having a coach who helps you through the tough levels of your healing journey.

And your friends and family? They're your cheer squad. Lean on them. Sometimes just talking it out with someone who listens can make a huge difference.

Exercises for Recovery: Rebuilding Yourself

Alright, it's time to start the healing process, both body and mind. Think of it as leveling up in your personal game of life.

1. **Mindfulness**: This is like hitting the pause button. Take a moment to just breathe. Sit somewhere quiet, focus on your breathing, and let your thoughts chill for a bit. It's all about being in the present, not the past.

2. **Journaling**: Consider your thoughts, feelings, fears, and hopes. It's like clearing the cache in your phone – it helps declutter your mind.

3. **Affirmations**: These are like your personal cheerleader chants. Repeat positive statements about yourself. "I am strong," "I am worthy of love," "I can heal." Say them out loud, write them down, believe in them.

4. **Therapeutic Activities**: This could be anything that makes you feel good – painting, playing music, skating, gaming, whatever floats your boat. It's about doing things that bring you joy and peace.

Remember, healing is a journey. It's okay to take it one step at a time. You've been through a lot, and it's totally normal to feel all sorts of emotions. But believe this – you're way stronger than you think, and with each day, you're getting even stronger. Keep pushing forward, and don't forget, you've got people rooting for you!

SPREAD KINDNESS LIKE CONFETTI

"Kindness is a language which the deaf can hear and the blind can see."

— MARK TWAIN

Ever heard the saying, "What goes around, comes around"? Well, it's time to sprinkle some kindness and watch it grow into some- thing beautiful. Here's a little secret: doing good for others doesn't just help them; it gives you a happiness boost, too!

Now, I've got a tiny but mighty favor to ask you...

Would you be willing to light up someone's world, someone you might not even know? Imagine them a bit like your younger self: eager to grow, hoping for change, and searching for a guiding light but not quite sure where to find it.

Our hearts and soul are poured into making recovery from toxic relationships a beacon of hope for everyone. Our dream? To spread this message far and wide. But we've got a small challenge: reaching every single person who needs this guide.

And here's where you, yes YOU, come in. Believe it or not, your voice is powerful. A lot of folks decide on a book based on what others say about it. So, on behalf of a teen navigating through a toxic relationships somewhere out there:

Your mission, should you choose to accept,: is to share your thoughts on this book.

This isn't about spending money. It's about donating a few moments of your time, which could forever alter the course of another teen's life. Your review has the magic to:

- ...help one more person feel understood and less alone.
- ...support someone in finding the courage to seek healthier rela- tionships.
- ...offer a lifeline to those drowning in doubt and confusion.
- ...inspire another soul to reclaim their confidence and happiness.
- ...turn someone's life story from despair to hope.

Feeling that warm glow inside already? To make your act of kind- ness a reality (in under a minute!), here's what to do:

leave a heartfelt review.

https://www.amazon.com/review/create-review/?ie=UTF8&channel=glance-detail&asin=

If the thought of helping a struggling teen out there makes your heart happy, you're definitely our kind of superhero. Welcome to the squad!

I'm super thrilled to embark on this journey with you toward a Toxic-Free Life with more confidence than you ever imagined. You're gonna be wowed by the guidance and insight waiting for you in the chapters ahead.

A million thanks for being awesome. Let's dive back into trans- forming lives together.

Just zap the QR code right here:

- Your cheerleader, Jordan Phoenix

9

SEXUAL ABUSE

WHAT IS SEXUAL ABUSE?

S exual abuse is really serious. It's when someone forces or pressures you into sexual stuff that you don't want. It's not just the obvious big bad things; it's any unwanted action that crosses your personal boundaries. This could be someone touching you in ways you don't want, pressuring you for nude photos, or making you feel uncomfortable with their words or actions.

Many people mistakenly believe that sexual abuse only has to do with going all the way – a penis in a vagina. But it's not, it involves any form of physical contact with your genitals. This includes touching, stroking, inserting things into a vagina (fingers, a penis, sex toys, or anything else), oral sex (with your/their mouth or tongue), and masturbation.

EMPOWERMENT AND AWARENESS

1. **Your Boundaries Matter:** Remember, your body belongs to you. You get to decide what's okay and what's not. If something doesn't feel right, it probably isn't. If you don't want to do something – you have the right not to do it! And no one in the world, I really mean *no one,* has the right to do anything to your body that you don't want. It doesn't matter what it is. It doesn't matter what else you did together, now or in the past. If there's something you don't want to do, and you say no, they must respect that no! If they do it anyway, that's sexual abuse.

2. **Consent is Everything:** Anything that happens should be totally okay with you. If you're feeling pressured or unsure, that's a big red flag. Consent should always be a clear and enthusiastic "Yes!"

3. **Speak Up, Stay Strong:** If someone's making you uncomfortable, it's okay to speak up. Saying "No" or "Stop" is your right, and it should always be respected.

4. **Safety First:** You deserve to feel safe and respected in all situations. If someone is making you feel otherwise, it's important to reach out to someone you trust – a teacher, parent, counselor, or a friend.

TYPES OF SEXUAL ABUSE

1. Unwanted touch, kisses, groping, etc.
2. Stripping you of clothes or parts of your clothing without your consent.
3. Coming into your bedroom/bathroom when you're undressed.

4. Installing malware on your computer or phone and using your webcam to spy on you when you're undressed or asleep in bed.
5. Physically forcing you to have sex.
6. Drugging you or intoxicating you so you'll have sex when you can't clearly make up your mind.
7. Having sex with you when you can't say yes or no (like if you're asleep).
8. Coercing you to have sex or making you feel guilty for not wanting to by saying things like: "That's what girlfriends do;" "If you loved me you would;" "You're such a prude;" "But we kissed! Now I need sex." "But you wanted it the other night," or, "But you did with your last boyfriend."
9. Threating to out you, hurt you, or spread rumors about you if you refuse to do what they want.
10. Not letting you use birth control or knowingly exposing you to HIV or other STDs.
11. Forcing you to have a baby or forcing you to terminate a pregnancy.

12. Forcing you to have sex with others.
13. Forcing you to watch pornography.
14. Demanding you sext.
15. Demanding nude pictures. An abusive partner might not say, "Sext me or else!" They might repeatedly ask you for nude pictures after you have said no by saying, "Please baby, don't you trust me? I just want something to look at when you're not here."

WHAT TO DO IF YOU WERE SEXUALLY ABUSED

Hey, I know this is really tough to talk about, but if you've been sexually abused, it's super important to take steps to take care of yourself. Here's what you can do:

1. **Find Someone to Talk To**: Talk to someone you trust, like a parent, teacher, or friend. You're not alone in this.
2. **Call the Police or a Hotline**: If you're in immediate danger, call 911. There are also hotlines you can call where people will listen and help.
3. **Get a Health Checkup**: It's important to make sure you're physically okay. A doctor can check you out and make sure everything's alright.
4. **Remember, It's Not Your Fault**: This is really important. What happened to you is not your fault. No matter what.

LEGAL AND ETHICAL CONSIDERATIONS

Here's a quick overview: Legally, sexual abuse is a serious crime. If you're underage, it's even more serious. Ethically, everyone should be treated with respect, and no one has the right to hurt you. If you're thinking about legal action, talking to a trusted adult or a lawyer can help you understand your options.

MYTHS AND MISCONCEPTIONS

There's a lot of wrong info out there about sexual abuse. Let's clear some things up:

Myth: "If you didn't say 'no,' it wasn't abuse."
Truth: If you didn't give a clear and enthusiastic "yes," it's abuse.

Myth: "Only girls can be victims."
Truth: Absolutely anyone can be a victim of sexual abuse, regard- less of gender.

Myth: "It's only abuse if it's physical."
Truth: Abuse can be physical, but it can also be words, pressure, or unwanted pictures and messages.

IMPACT ON VICTIMS

Survivors of sexual abuse can feel a whole bunch of ways. Physically, it can hurt. Emotionally, you might feel scared, sad, or even angry. Psychologically, it can be confusing and hard to deal with. It's okay to have all these feelings.

Societal Perspectives and Stigma

Society sometimes has weird views about sexual abuse, like victim-blaming or not taking it seriously. This can make it hard to talk about. But remember, more and more people understand how serious this is and are there to support you.

Always remember, you're strong, you're brave, and you have the right to be safe and respected. Take it one step at a time.

HEALING AND MOVING FORWARD

Healing from sexual abuse is a personal journey, and it takes time. Acknowledge your feelings and know that it's okay to seek help.

Talking to a counselor or therapist can really help in understanding and working through your feelings.

Healing is about rediscovering your strength and realizing that what happened doesn't define you. You're much more than that.

Remember:

- You're not alone in this.
- What happened isn't your fault. You are a good person. What happened does not define your worth or your future.
- You have the right to feel safe and be respected.
- You have the right over your body – always!
- You have the right to say no.
- You deserve to have a good, happy future.

Take your time, be kind to yourself, and reach out when you're ready. You're strong, and you can get through this.

10

HEALTHY PHYSICAL INTIMACY AND SEX

When it comes to sex, especially in teen relationships, there's a lot to understand about what's healthy and what's not. Healthy sex is about mutual respect, comfort, and consent. It's a caring and kind experience where both partners feel safe, happy, and respected. The key here is that both of you are on the same page and feel good about what's happening.

Healthy sex is never about fear, control, or pain. It's not about one person being dominant or using force. If one person feels scared, hurt, or pressured, that's a big red flag. It's not normal or okay for sex to be painful or frightening. In a caring relationship, both part- ners pay attention to each other's comfort and boundaries. They communicate openly about what they like and what they don't, always making sure that each other feels safe and valued.

It's super important to know that what you might see in movies, read in books, or even come across online isn't always a picture of what healthy, consensual sex looks like.

Some people watch videos where the girl is strangled, knocked about, thrown onto a bed, suffocated, and insulted. They think that's how sex is – but it's not. That's abuse, and it's not good or healthy.

Real-life intimacy is about caring for each other's feelings, desires, and well-being. It's totally okay to take things slow, to say no, and to have clear boundaries. And remember, sex should always be a mutual decision, never something that one person feels pressured or forced into.

Understanding this can make a huge difference in your rela- tion- ships and your well-being. Knowing what healthy physical inti- macy looks like helps you make choices that are right for you, choices that make you feel good, not scared or hurt. Remember, you have the right to feel safe and respected, always.

11

GL AMORIZED TOXIC REL ATIONSHIPS

Ever seen those movies or read those books where the hot guy is all broody and intense, and sometimes he's kinda mean or even rough with the girl, but it's portrayed as super romantic? It's like, the more he pushes her away or gets jealous, the more he hurts her, the more passionate their love seems. But here's the real talk: this isn't cool, hot, or romantic. It's actually really messed up.

First off, let's talk about what's often glamorized in these stories. Like, when a guy gets all possessive or jealous, and it's shown as him just being super into the girl. Or when he's straight-up mean, insulting, or even physically rough (shaking, smacking, strangling, bruising), but it's twisted into some sign of his 'deep feelings.' Or like when he forces himself upon her, and it's brushed off as a sign of passion?

That's not passion, my friend. That's abuse.

In real life, love isn't about being hurt, insulted, or forced into anything, especially not sex. Love is about respect, kindness, and caring for each other's feelings and boundaries. If someone truly loves you, they won't want to hurt you or control you. They'll want to lift you up, not bring you down. They won't want to 'own' you or enslave you to them. That's an abusive control freak, not a loving partner.

Now, why is it important to understand this? Because when you grow up reading these stories or watching these movies, you might start thinking that's what love looks like. That it's normal for rela- tionships to be hurtful or abusive. But here's the thing – it's not.

Abuse is never a sign of love or passion. If someone is hurting you, whether physically or emotionally, that's a red flag. It's not roman- tic. It's dangerous.

In real life, being with someone who's abusive can be really scary and hurtful. It's not like the movies where everything magically gets better (or where she also turns into a vampire and they live happily ever after). It can leave you feeling scared, sad, and alone.

So, how can you tell if a relationship is healthy or not? Look for respect, honesty, and kindness. In a healthy relationship, you feel safe to be yourself, you're not scared of your partner, and you don't have to put up with being hurt or insulted.

If you feel unhappy in your relationship, that's a major red flag.

Remember, you deserve to be treated with love and respect, always. Don't let those glamorized stories trick you into thinking otherwise. Real love lifts you up; it doesn't tear you down.

PASSION IN HEALTHY RELATIONSHIPS

Passion is that fire you feel in a relationship, right? It's intense, it's exciting, and it can make you feel really alive. But here's the thing: true passion is about deep connection and enthusiasm, not about control or harm. When someone's truly passionate about their partner, they show it through affection, respect, and genuine interest in their well-being. They might plan special dates, listen intently to what their partner says, and show their love in thoughtful ways. It's about sharing excitement and happiness, not about exerting control or power.

JEALOUSY IS NOT LOVE

Jealousy, on the other hand, is a whole different ball game. It's often mistaken for passion or love, but trust me, they're not the same thing. Jealousy is about insecurity and fear – it's the fear of losing someone or feeling threatened by others. While a little bit of jealousy can be natural, it's not healthy when it turns into posses- siveness or control. Love is about trust and security, not about feeling like you have to keep someone on a tight leash. In healthy relationships, partners trust each other and give each other space to be their own person.

PHYSICAL VIOLENCE AND INTIMACY

Now, let's talk about physical violence, especially in intimate moments like some of those wild vampire novels suggest. When things get rough or violent, like someone being thrown down or hurt, it's not passion – it's abuse. This idea that a guy is so 'over- come with passion' that he can't control himself and gets violent? That's just plain wrong. Scientifically, being turned on doesn't

make someone violent. That kind of behavior comes from a place of wanting to control or dominate, not from love or arousal.

HEALTHY EXPRESSIONS OF PASSION AND LOVE

So, what does healthy passion look like in a relationship? It's about showing your love and excitement in ways that respect your part- ner's boundaries. It's about being gentle, caring, and considerate. A kind and loving boyfriend might show his passion by holding his partner close, by being attentive to her needs and comfort, and by making sure she feels safe and cherished. It's about mutual respect and making sure both partners feel good, not just one.

Remember, in a healthy relationship, love is about caring, respect, and making each other feel safe and valued. Anything that hurts, scares, or makes someone feel uncomfortable isn't love or passion – it's a red flag to be aware of. Love lifts you up; it doesn't bring you down.

When things get dark and painful, instead of leaving a toxic relationship, here are the 7 common things peeps do(spoiler: they don't help!).

It's like almost everyone tries these 7 common ways to escape their dark maze – but they always lead them right back into an even darker part of it!

Let's take a look at what these 7 failed ways are:

1. **Asking Only Your Friends for Advice**: Okay, so it's super normal to chat with your squad about relationship probs. But sometimes, they might not have all the answers (no offense to them!). They're figuring things out just like you, so their advice might not always be the most solid.

2. **Playing the Ignore Game**: Pretending everything's chill and hoping the probs will magically disappear? Spoiler: They won't. Ignoring the issues means they'll just keep piling up *and getting worse*. It's like ignoring a messy room – the mess doesn't clean itself, right?

3. **Mission 'Change Them'**: If you're trying to turn your partner into someone they're not... well, that's mission impossible. People only change if they

really want to. You can't force someone to be different, just like you can't force a cat to start barking.

4. **Rebound Rush**: Jumping into a new relationship right after a toxic one? That's like finishing a marathon and immediately running another. Give your heart some time to chill and heal. You don't want to end up in another messy situation because you didn't take a break.

5. **Playing Detective**: Constantly checking up on them to see if they've changed or what they're up to? That's like rewatching a bad movie and hoping the ending will be different. Spoiler: it won't.

6. **Making Excuses for Their Behavior**: If you find yourself saying things like "They're just stressed" or "They didn't mean it," you might be making excuses for behavior that isn't cool. Remember, actions speak louder than words. Abuse is NEVER okay and you never have to tolerate it no matter what their 'reason' is.

7. **Waiting for a Fairytale Fix**: Thinking things will magically get better or waiting for a fairytale ending? Real life isn't a movie. Solutions take work, and sometimes, the best move is to step away from what's hurting you.

Remember, getting out of a toxic relationship is tough but super important for your well-being. You deserve someone who treats you right, not someone who makes you feel like you're in a never- ending drama series.

RECOGNIZING YOUR PART IN THE TOXIC DANCE

Let's get real for a sec. Sometimes in relationships, it's not just about the other person being toxic – it's also about why we stick around.

It's like we're doing this dance, but the steps are all off. They keep treading on your toes, but you keep on dancing with them.

Maybe you find yourself making excuses for them, or you keep hoping they'll change. Or maybe you're scared to be alone. It's important to recognize your part in this dance, so you can start changing the steps.

THE ATTRACTION TO TOXIC RELATIONSHIPS

Ever wonder why sometimes we're drawn to people who aren't good for us? It's kinda like being addicted to a bad TV show – you know it's not great, but you can't stop watching. Sometimes it's because the drama feels exciting, or maybe it's what we've seen in movies and think it's how love should be. Or, it might be deeper stuff, like low self-esteem or past experiences that make us think this is what we deserve. Understanding this attraction is key to turning off the show and finding something better.

BREAKING THE CYCLE OF TOXIC REL ATIONSHIPS

Okay, so you recognize the dance, and you get why you're drawn to it. Now what? Breaking the cycle isn't easy, but it's so worth it. Start by building up your self-love and self-respect. Remember, you're awesome and deserve someone who treats you right. Spend time with friends who lift you up, dive into hobbies that make you happy, and maybe talk to a counselor or therapist. It's all about creating a new dance for yourself, one where you're leading and not just following along.

FINDING YOUR RHYTHM OUTSIDE THE TOXIC TANGO

It's time to take a step back, look at your relationship dance, and decide if it's really the one you want to be in. It's about under- standing your worth and finding the courage to change the music to something that truly makes you happy. You've got the power to choose your dance, your way.

You're stronger than you think, and capable of amazing things – including finding a healthy, happy relationship that's just right for you. Keep believing in yourself, and remember, the best dances are the ones where you feel free and joyous. You got this!

12

DRAWING THE LINE: SET TING BOUNDARIES LIKE A BOSS

Okay, so have you ever seen a magic show where the magician pulls a rabbit out of a hat and thought, "Whoa, how cool would it be to do that?" Well, guess what? You've got your own kind of magic trick up your sleeve, and it's all about setting boundaries in relationships. It's like having a superpower to make people respect your space, your time, and your vibes. No rabbits or hats needed, just pure, empowering boundary-setting magic. Let's dive in!

SAYING " NO" LIKE A PRO

Ever had that moment when a friend's like, "Can you help me out?" and inside, you're screaming "No way!" but you end up saying "Sure"?

We've all been there. Saying 'Yes' when you really wanna say 'No' – it's like a reflex, especially when you're worried about letting someone down or what they'll think.

But here's the real talk: saying 'No' doesn't make you a bad person, bad friend, or selfish. It makes you someone who knows their limits. That's where assertiveness training enters the chat. Think of it as a workout for your communication muscles. It's about getting comfy with expressing what you really think and feel, minus the guilt trip. It's about flexing your 'No' muscle and feeling good about it.

SELF-RESPECT: YOUR VIP PASS TO BOUNDARIES

Picture this: You're at a concert, and they start playing a song that's deafeningly loud and sounds like nails on a chalkboard. Would you stick around, cringing and hurting? Nah, you'd probably bounce until the song's over. Why? 'Cause you respect yourself enough not to sit through something that's literally painful.

That's what self-respect is all about. It's knowing you're worth it and treating yourself right. Setting boundaries? That's a major part of self-respect. It's like saying, "Hey, my time and energy are precious, and I'm not just gonna let anyone mess with that." It's about knowing your worth and making sure everyone else knows it too.

Setting up Your Boundary Game

A boundary is all about standing your ground and knowing you're totally worth it. You're the director of your own life, and it's time to call the shots. Get ready to transform your relationships and treat yourself like the rockstar you are.

Setting boundaries isn't just smart; it's essential. It's about making sure you're treated the way you deserve, in friendships, in love, everywhere. You've got this, and it's going to be amazing!

Emotional Health: The Video Game of Your Mind

Think of your emotional health like a super immersive video game. Positive emotions are like power-ups – joy, love, happiness, peace – they boost your energy and help you level up. Negative emotions? They're like those tricky obstacles or annoying enemies – stress, guilt, resentment, anger – trying to bring you down.

If you keep ignoring your boundaries, it's like letting those baddies overrun your game. Setting and maintaining boundaries? That's like strategizing and using your best moves to keep the game under control. It's all about protecting your mental space by making sure your game stays fun, positive, and totally winnable.

Identifying Personal Limits: Your Game, Your Rules

Alright, let's talk about your fave ice cream flavor. It's like your go- to comfort food, right? Now imagine that someone says you can't have it anymore. No way! Just like you have your ice cream prefer- ences, you have personal limits in relationships, too.

Identifying your personal limits is like creating your own game settings. It's about figuring out what you're cool with and what's a no-go, what makes you feel good, and what's a total energy- drainer. Think about your past and present relationships – what's made you happy, what's made you feel uneasy? These are your clues to setting up your own rela- tionship 'game rules.'

Expressing Boundaries: Clear Communication FTW

Ever been in a restaurant and got served the wrong order? You'd let the waiter know, right? Same goes for relationships. If some- one's stepping over your line, you gotta let them know.

Expressing your boundaries is like placing your order clearly. It's all about communicating what you need, what you expect, and where your limits are in a way that's direct but cool. Use 'I' state- ments like "I feel uneasy when..." or "I need some space to..." to keep it about your needs, not about blaming anyone else.

Game On: Navigating Relationships with Boundaries

Setting boundaries in relationships is like being the boss of your own game. You set the level, you choose the challenges, and you decide how to play. Remember, clear communication and respecting your own rules are key to a healthy, happy relationship game.

Keep playing your game your way, respecting your needs and feel- ings. You're the hero in this adventure, and with the right strate- gies, you'll totally ace it. Game on!

Dealing with Boundary Violations: The Frisbee in the Park Scenario

Okay, picture this: You're chilling in the park, soaking up the sun, when suddenly – bam! – a frisbee crashes onto your picnic blan- ket, messing up your snacks. What do you do? Just like in this scenario, when someone crosses your bound- aries in real life, it's kinda like that frisbee invasion. It throws off your groove and invades your space.

Handling boundary violations is like picking up that frisbee and giving it back. You gotta address the issue calmly. It's not about starting a fight; it's about letting them know, "Hey, that wasn't cool."

When someone oversteps, again, use 'I' statements to express how you feel, like "I felt hurt when you..." or "I didn't appre- ciate when..." Clear, calm, and straight-up.

Consistency in Upholding Boundaries: Like Riding a Bike

Ever tried learning to ride a bike? It's all wobbly at first, right? But with practice, you get the hang of it. Upholding boundaries is pretty much the same deal. It takes practice, patience, and a whole lot of sticking to your guns.

Being consistent with your boundaries is like keeping those bike wheels turning. You gotta stay firm, even if it feels tough or awkward – or if people push back. It's all about showing that your boundaries are legit – no backpedaling.

If you start doubting yourself, just remember why you set these boundaries. Think about that peace of mind, that feeling of being in control, that respect for your own space. That's your drive, your why, your reason to keep those boundaries strong.

Setting boundaries isn't a one-and-done kind of thing. It's an ongoing process, kinda like updating your playlist as your music taste changes. It's about creating a vibe of respect and open communication in all your relationships. And hey, it's totally cool to tweak your boundaries as you grow, 'cause they're yours to draw and redraw as you see fit.

So, keep drawing those lines in the sand of your personal space. You've got the stick, and you totally know how to use it. Set those boundaries and ride that bike like a boss. You got this!

Respecting Your Own Boundaries: The Personal Fortress

Think of yourself as this epic fortress in your favorite video game. Your boundaries? They're like the walls and defenses that keep the baddies out and protect the awesome stuff inside. To build these defenses, you've gotta know your fortress like the back of your hand – what makes it strong, what needs extra guarding, and all the cool stuff it holds.

Self-awareness is like having the ultimate game guide for your fortress. It means understanding your needs, your values, your emotions, and what gives you strength. It's about figuring out what keeps your fortress safe and what makes it thrive. So, take a moment to think: What do you need in your relationships? What are your deal-breakers? What gets you fired up?

Knowing all this stuff is key to setting up your boundaries. And remember, your fortress is one-of-a-kind. What works for others might not work for you, and that's totally okay. Embrace your uniqueness – it's what makes your fortress epic.

Self-Care: The Ultimate Fortress Upkeep

Now, picture your fortress facing a mega storm – we're talking lightning, thunder, the works. To keep standing strong, it needs some serious TLC. That's where self-care comes into play.

Self-care is like the ultimate maintenance crew for your fortress. It's about taking care of your body with good food and rest, keeping your mind sharp with positive vibes and learning, and feeding your soul with things that make you happy. Every time you do something good for yourself, it's like adding an extra layer of protection to your fortress.

Practicing self-care isn't selfish; it's essential. It's making sure your fortress – aka you – is ready to take on whatever the game of life throws at you. So go ahead, treat yourself to that smoothie, take that chill day, read that cool book, or go for that invigorating run. Every bit of self-care is a power-up for your personal boundaries.

Leveling Up in the Game of Boundaries

Setting and respecting your own boundaries is like leveling up in the most important game – your life. You're the hero of this story, and your fortress is your domain. Keep it strong, keep it safe, and keep rocking it your way.

NAVIGATING THE KINGDOM OF LIFE

Imagine your life is like a bustling video game kingdom. You've got allies and foes, friendly NPCs, and some not-so-friendly charac- ters. To really ace this game, it's not just about having the strongest fortress. What you need is some serious skills – like emotional intelligence.

Emotional Intelligence: Your In-Game Guide

Think of emotional intelligence as your wise in-game guide or advisor. It's all about getting to know your own emotions and understanding the feelings of other players in the game. It's like having this superpower to use your emotional smarts to make better decisions, adapt to different situations, and even level up in your quests.

Say a friend in the game – IRL, we're talking – crosses a boundary. If you've got emotional intelligence, you'd first tune into how that makes you feel. Then, you'd try to see where they're coming from, kinda empathize with their side of the story. And finally, you'd communicate your boundary in a way that's clear but totally respectful.

Building Bridges, Not Just Walls

By leveling up your emotional intelligence, you're doing more than just protecting your fortress. You're also building bridges – bridges of understanding, respect, and shared growth. It's not just about keeping others out; it's about connecting with them in a way that respects your boundaries.

Your Power-Ups: Self-Awareness, Self-Care, Emotional Intelligence

So here's the deal: Respecting your own boundaries isn't just about one thing. It's this combo of self-awareness (knowing your charac- ter), self-care (upgrading your stats), and emotional intelligence (mastering the social side of the game). Each one's like a unique power-up, but together? They make you unstoppable.

These power-ups don't isolate you in the game; they give you the space to explore, level up, and be the true hero of your story. So cherish these skills, honor your boundaries, and respect the power they give you. 'Cause in the grand game of life, they're not just tools – they're what make you a legend.

Remember, in the epic adventure that is life, you're the main char- acter. Your boundaries are your strengths, your power-ups, your magic. Embrace them, and watch as you conquer quests and win battles. Game on!

How to Totally Rock at Respecting Others' Boundaries

Imagine you're at this awesome open mic night, and there's a singer just killing it on stage. You're not just hearing the music; you're getting the whole story, the emotions, the vibe. That's active listening, and it's like the ultimate respect move in your daily talks.

Active listening? It's about really being there in the convo. It's tuning into the unsaid stuff, the feels behind the words, the little signals. It's showing the other person that you get them, that their words and boundaries are important to you.

Next time you're chatting with someone, put your own thoughts on hold for a sec. Really listen to what they're saying, how they're saying it, and even what their body language is throwing down. Active listening isn't just about nodding along; it's about really getting where they're coming from.

Empathy: The Heart-to-Heart Connection

You know those moments when you're feeling down and a friend just gets it? That's empathy in action. It's like this superpower that lets you connect heart-to-heart, feeling what they're feeling.

Empathy is about slipping into someone else's shoes, checking out their view of the world, and really feeling what they're going through. It's about getting their boundaries, where they're comfy and where they're not, and what pushes their buttons. It's about feeling their feels, even if you don't totally agree with them.

So, when you bump into someone's boundaries, don't just nod and move on. Try to feel why they've set them up. Understand their need for space or respect. Empathy is more than just respecting boundaries; it's about celebrating their entire human vibe.

Respect for Personal Space: The Breathing Room Rule

Ever been on a super crowded bus and felt like you needed a bubble of your own space? Yeah, imagine feeling that cramped in your relationships. Not cool, right?

Respecting personal space is all about giving people room to do their thing, to grow, to just be. Everyone's got their comfort zone, their space needs, their own set of boundaries.

Next time you're hanging out with someone, be mindful of how much space they need. Let them express themselves, let them stretch out, let them feel respected. When you respect someone's personal space, you're not just saying, "I see your boundaries;" you're saying, "I celebrate you being you."

Wrapping It Up: The Art of Boundary Respect

Getting good at respecting others' boundaries is like leveling up in the game of relationships. It's about active listening, feeling empa- thy, and giving space. It's about recognizing that just like you, everyone's got their unique space needs and boundaries. So go ahead, be that person who not just respects but cherishes the boundaries of others. It's your way of saying, "You're awesome, just the way you are."

Remember, every relationship is a two-way street. The more you respect others' boundaries, the more you'll find your own being respected. It's all about balance, understanding, and mutual respect. You got this!

ACCEPTANCE OF DIFFERENCES: THE ULTIMATE FLOWER POWER

Picture a garden with only roses. Pretty, right? But now, imagine a garden bursting with all kinds of flowers – roses, daisies, sunflow- ers, tulips. So much more awesome, isn't it? That's the beauty of diversity, of different vibes all coming together.

Accepting differences is like vibing with this rainbow garden. It's about understanding that everyone's unique, with their own thoughts, feels, life stories, and boundaries. It's not about dissing these differences or trying to change them; it's about celebrating them.

The next time you meet someone whose boundaries are different from yours, don't be all judge-y. Instead, throw a party for their uniqueness, their individual vibe, their personal space rules. Accepting differences isn't just about respecting boundaries; it's about high-fiving diversity.

The Compass of Respect: Your Guide to Boundary Awesomeness

So here's the deal: Respecting boundaries is like having this super cool compass in your life's journey. Each direction has its own magic:

- **North (Active Listening)**: This is your guide to really getting others, tuning into their words, and understanding what's behind them.
- **East (Empathy)**: This path leads you to feel what others feel, to really connect heart-to-heart.
- **West (Respecting Personal Space)**: This reminds you to give people the room they need to be their awesome selves.
- **South (Accepting Differences)**: This inspires you to celebrate everyone's unique colors and flavors.

With this compass in your hands, you're not just navigating the map of respecting boundaries; you're on a voyage to healthier, happier, and more respectful relationships.

Setting Sail on Your Respectful Relationship Voyage

Keep this compass close, trust where it leads, and remember: every step you take towards respecting others' boundaries is like planting a new, beautiful flower in the garden of life. Ready to continue the journey? Let's sail towards a world where every unique flower is celebrated and respected.

Always remember, in the beautiful garden of life, every flower has its place, its beauty, its worth. Embracing and respecting these differences make the garden so much more vibrant. You got this, and the journey's going to be amazing!

13

SAYING ' NO' RESPECTFULLY

YOUR RIGHT, YOUR CHOICE

In the wild world of being a teen, knowing how to say 'no' is super important. It's like having a secret shield that protects your time, your body, and your choices. Saying 'no' doesn't make you a bad friend or uncool; it's about respecting yourself and your boundaries. Let's explore what 'saying no' really means and why it's totally okay to do it.

What Does Saying No Mean?

Saying 'no' is like drawing a line in the sand. It's telling others, "This is where my comfort zone ends." It's not about rejecting the person asking; it's about being true to yourself. It means you're in charge of your decisions, whether it's about your time, your body, your actions, or your feelings.

Example Scenarios IRL

- **The Unwanted Hangout:** Your friend wants to hang out, but you're exhausted. Saying, "I really need some downtime tonight, can we raincheck?" shows that you value your rest and it's okay to prioritize it.
- **Peer Pressure Party:** You're at a party, and someone offers you a drink you're not comfortable with. A firm "No thanks, I'm good with what I have" is your right. It's about staying true to what feels right for you.
- **Uncomfortable Touch:** Someone wants a hug, but you're not a touchy-feely person. "I'm not really into hugs, but I'm glad to see you!" keeps it light and friendly while respecting your personal space.
- **Group Study Overload:** Your study group wants to meet, but you've got too much on your plate. "I can't make it this time; I've got to focus on another project" is a respectful way to manage your time.
- **Relationship Boundaries:** Your partner wants to take things to the next level, but you're not ready. "I really like you, but I'm not ready for that step yet," is honest and fair to both of you.

CONSENT: IT' S A BIG DEAL

Consent is like a VIP pass; it's needed for anything that involves you, especially when it comes to your body and choices. It's saying 'yes' or 'no' to things like physical touch, what you eat or drink, or any activity. Remember, if it's not a clear, enthusiastic 'yes,' it's a 'no.'

Saying No Respectfully

It's not just about what you say but how you say it. An aggressive 'no' sounds angry, accusative, and loud like "No! How dare you ask me to babysit?"

A respectful 'no' can sound like, "I appreciate you asking, but I'm not comfortable with that," or "Thanks for thinking of me, but that's not really my thing." It's clear, it's kind, and it's firm.

Reacting Respectfully When Someone Says No

If someone tells you 'no,' respect it like a stop sign. It's not about you; it's about their comfort zone. A cool response is, "No prob- lem, thanks for letting me know!" It shows you respect their choice and keeps things positive.

Final Thoughts: Your Life, Your Rules

Your life is yours, and saying 'no' is part of steering it in the direc- tion you want. It doesn't make you selfish or unlik- able; it makes you the boss of your own life. Respect your own no and the no of others, and watch how it changes things for the better. You've got this!

" I ' M AFRAID TO LEAVE!"

T otally get it. Leaving a toxic relationship can feel like the hardest level in a video game, but it's a game you gotta win

for yourself. Here's the real talk on how to power through:

Why It's Tough to Let Go: Okay, so leaving a toxic relationship is super hard, especially when you're a teen. Everything feels like the end of the world, right? You might be scared of being solo, thinking you won't find anyone else. Or freaking out about what life looks like after you say goodbye. Plus, if it's your first major breakup, you're like, "How do I even deal with this?"

Kick Fear to the Curb: First up, gather your squad. Friends, fam, even peeps in online communities like r/teenrelationships can be lifelines. Share your story, listen to theirs. It helps, promise. Next, dive into something new. Start a hobby, join a club, volunteer – it's all about getting your mind off things and feeling good about yourself. And hey, if the fear feels too heavy, reach out for pro help, like Teen Line. They've got your back.

Positive Vibes Only: Use affirmations and dream up a way better future. Imagine a relationship where you're treated right. It's out there waiting for you.

Handling the Feels Post-Breakup: Post-toxic-relationship, you're gonna feel a whole mess of emotions. Sad, mad, confused – it's all normal. Try EFT/Tapping or repeat some cool affirmations to ease the ache. Missing your ex? Totally normal too, even if things were rough.

Strategies to Soothe Your Soul: Journaling can be a huge help. Just pour all those feelings into words, either in an app like Penzu or old-school with pen and paper. Physical activity is also a big mood booster. Whether it's sports, yoga, or just chilling in nature, it'll help clear your head. Meditation's another great tool. Apps like Calm or Headspace have special stuff just for us teens.

Remember, healing from a toxic relationship is a journey, not a sprint. Be kind to yourself and give yourself the time you need to heal and grow. You've got this!

Alright, let's talk about sparking some hope for your future love life after you've dealt with a toxic relationship. I know, thinking about jumping back into the dating pool can be kinda scary, but let's break it down:

Why It's Scary to Think About New Relationships: Post-toxic- relationship life can make you super cautious about starting some- thing new. You might be freaked out about going through the same drama again or not spotting the warning signs early enough. It's totally normal to feel this way.

Hope's Not Just a Four-Letter Word: Remember, not every rela- tionship is going to be a rerun of the bad stuff. Your past doesn't have to be a shadow over your future.

Easy Does It: When you're ready to dip your toes back into the dating scene, take it slow. No rush. Get to know the person, see how they act in different situations. It's like checking out the trailer before you watch the whole movie.

Raise the Bar: Set those standards high. You deserve someone who treats you right – with respect, kindness, and all that good stuff. Check out @respectyourself on Insta for some daily doses of how awesome you are and how you should be treated.

Learn and Grow: Your past relationship? It's not just a bad memory; it's a lesson. Use it to figure out what you're so not cool with in a relationship. Red flags? You'll spot 'em from a mile away now.

Building hope for the future is all about believing that you deserve the best, learning from the past, and moving forward at your own pace. You've got a whole future of awesome relationships ahead of you. Just believe in yourself and take it one step at a time. You've totally got this!

EXITING A TOXIC RELATIONSHIP

STEPPING INTO THE SUNLIGHT

Escaping the Dark Maze: Your First Brave Step

Imagine you're in this super dark maze, feeling totally lost and trapped. It feels like there's no way out, just endless twisty paths and dead ends. You're filled with fear, feeling suffocated, haunted, followed, like you're in a horror movie. Like nothing will ever get better and you're doomed to be here forever.

But then, you spot this door. You try it and find it's unlocked.

You hesitate. It's kinda scary, right? The idea of opening it and not knowing what's on the other side. But you're so over this dark, depressing maze. You can't take living in it anymore.

So, you push the door open and

–

whoa – it's like stepping into a whole new world. Bright sunshine, lush green fields, flowers everywhere, people laughing and splashing in a lake. It's like going from a black-and-white movie into full-on color.

You start walking, leaving that dark maze behind. With each step, the heaviness starts lifting. The fear, the stress, the feeling of being stuck – it all starts fading away. And before you know it, you're laughing, playing with the others, soaking up those warm sunbeams. You feel happy, free, confident, and loved. Your new friends are kind and caring. You enjoy spending time with them. Life suddenly feels like it's worth living. The way your new friends are treating you, like you're special and lovable makes you feel like 'maybe there's actually nothing wrong with me after all...'

Your days are fun and happy. Your future is hopeful and

bright. You feel like you have something worth living for again. After a few days, you're smiling and laughing again.

Someone asks if you'd ever go back to that torturous dark maze, and you're like, "No way, not in a million years!"

That's what it feels like to walk away from a toxic relationship. Scary at first, but once you step out, it's the best thing ever. It's like you've been given a brand-new life – happier, freer, calmer. You'll wonder why you didn't open that door sooner.

Ready to Open the Door?

So here you are, standing in front of that door, ready to step out of the nightmare maze and into a new, brighter chapter. It's a big leap, leaving the familiar behind and facing the unknown. But it's also the most freeing thing you'll ever do.

This chapter is all about making that leap. We'll talk about facing the tough stuff head-on, planning your way out, cutting ties, and dealing with what comes next. It's not just about leaving the bad behind; it's about embracing all the good waiting for you.

So, are you ready to peek outside and see the amazing world that's waiting? Let's do this together. One step at a time, we'll leave the darkness behind and step into a life full of light, laughter, and endless possibilities.

Remember, you're the hero of your story, and every hero deserves a happy ending. The door's right there, and a brighter, happier life is just on the other side. You've got the courage, the strength, and the power to open it. Let's turn this page together and start a new, amazing journey. You ready? Let's leap!

MASTERING THE ART OF CONFRONTATION: PLAYING IT SMART

Ever played a game of chess? Every move is crucial, right? That's kinda like dealing with conflicts. It's this careful game where what you do or say can either ramp things up or cool them down.

Whether you're dealing with a disagreement with your squad or a clash with your partner, think of it more like a puzzle to solve, not a battle to win. Here are some pro gamer moves:

- **Pause for a Timeout**: When emotions are all over the place, hit that pause button. Give yourself a moment to chill and strategize, just like planning your next chess move.
- **'I' Statements for the Win**: Instead of going all "You did this," try "I feel this way." Like, say "I feel bummed when our plans get canceled last minute," not "You're always ditching me!"
- **Get Their Perspective**: Before you respond, try to get where they're coming from. It's like checking out their side of the chessboard to make a smarter move.

NON-VIOLENT COMMUNICATION: THE L ANGUAGE OF CHILL

Non-violent communication is like learning a whole new language – one that's all about being cool, respectful, and understanding. Here's the breakdown:

- **Just the Facts**: Start with what actually happened, no extra drama. Like, "I noticed you were late to our hangout..."
- **Feel Your Feels**: Share how it made you feel. "It kinda made me feel let down..."
- **Name Your Needs**: Let them know what you need from them. "I need to know I can count on our plans..."
- **Make a Request**: Finish with something clear and doable. "Could we agree on times and stick to them?"

EMOTIONAL REGUL ATION: SMOOTH DRIVING ON BUMPY ROADS

Emotional regulation is like having awesome shock absorbers in your car. It helps you ride smoothly over the emotional bumps of confrontation.

Try these tactics:

- **Deep Breathing**: Slow, deep breaths can seriously help calm your mind.

- **Stay Mindful**: Keep your mind in the now, not stuck in the past or stressing about the future.
- **Positive Self-Talk**: Be your own cheerleader. Remind yourself that it's okay to be upset and that you've totally got this.

Wrapping It Up: Confrontation, But Make It Cool

Mastering the art of confrontation is all about playing it smart, calm, and respectful. It's about navigating through those tricky moments like a pro, keeping your cool, and finding solutions that work for everyone. You're the player with the controller, and with these skills, you're ready to win any game life throws at you.

Remember, confrontation doesn't have to be a downer. It's an opportunity to grow, understand, and level up in your relation- ships. You've got the skills, now go and play the game like the champ you are!

CRAFTING YOUR ESCAPE PLAN: GAME PLAN FOR FREEDOM

Safety First: Your Shield in Rough Times

Picture you're gearing up for an epic adventure, like climbing a mountain. You'd pack your essentials, check the forecast, and plan your route, right? That's exactly what you gotta do when planning to leave a toxic relationship. It's all about being prepared and keeping yourself safe.

First off, check out the risks. Could things get nasty when you break it off? Like, could they try to hurt you or follow you around? If so, you need a safety shield. This could mean looping in your parents, a teacher, or another adult you trust. If things could get really serious, maybe even involve the police.

Get a safe spot lined up, like a friend's house or a relative's place, somewhere your soon-to-be-ex doesn't know about. It's super important to have a safe hideout.

And hey, if you've shared passwords with your partner, change 'em all. Do it at night when they're asleep, and block them on all your accounts. Take back your digital space.

Your Squad: Your Ultimate Support Network

Think of your fave group adventure movie. It's always about friends sticking together through thick and thin, right? Exiting a toxic relationship is kinda like that. You need your own squad – friends, fam, teachers, anyone who's got your back.

Make a list of peeps you can rely on. Reach out, share what you're comfy with, and let them know you might need a shoulder or a helping hand. You'll be amazed at how many people are ready to step up.

Consider joining a support group, too. Connecting with others who've been through similar stuff can be super helpful. They get it, and they can share their own tips and tricks.

And don't forget about getting some pro advice. A counselor or therapist can be a game-changer. They've got the know-how to help you navigate this tricky path.

The Journey Ahead: Stepping Into Your New Chapter

Crafting your exit strategy from a toxic relationship is like plan- ning for the most important journey of your life. It might seem daunting, scary even, but it's also the path to your freedom. With your safety plan, your trusty squad, and the right support, you're ready to cross that bridge to a brighter, healthier future.

Remember, you're the hero of your story, and every hero deserves a happy, safe, and fulfilling journey. Plan carefully, lean on your squad, and take that brave first step. The road ahead is yours to conquer. Let's do this!

LEGAL CONSIDERATIONS: THE ROADMAP TO SAFETY

First up, if there's been any form of abuse in your relation-ship, like if things got physical or super scary, it's mega important to let the authorities know. This isn't just about you; it's about keeping everyone safe.

Dealing with legal stuff can feel super overwhelming, espe-cially when you're already in an emotional whirlwind. But think of it like a roadmap in your escape plan. It's there to make sure you're headed in the right direction – towards safety and freedom.

Your Journey, Your Pace

Remember, leaving a toxic relationship isn't about rushing to some imaginary finish line. It's about moving at a pace that feels right for you, making sure you're safe, and having people around who've got your back.

It's all about knowing your rights and making choices that are best for you. Sure, it might seem like a giant mountain to climb, but every step you take is a step closer to a happier, healthier you. You've got this. You're stronger than you realize and way braver than you think.

THE BREAKUP: CHOOSING YOUR PATH

Imagine you're at this big crossroads. The path you've been on? It's coming to an end, and now it's time to pick a new direction. Breaking up is just like that. And having a clear, honest chat is your compass to guide you.

It's about being clear and kind when you express your decision. Plan out what you need to say. Be real, but be gentle. Instead of blaming, focus on expressing your feelings and what you need. Like, say, "I feel like I need more space to grow," instead of "You're holding me back."

It's not the easiest convo, but it's a crucial one. Clear communica- tion isn't just about ending things; it's about kicking off a new chapter of your life with clarity and peace.

Moving Forward: Your New Adventure

Crafting your escape plan and facing the breakup – it's all part of your journey to a better, brighter life. It's about taking control, finding your voice, and stepping into a future where you're the one calling the shots. Plan with care, speak with heart, and walk confi- dently towards the new chapter waiting for you.

Remember, this journey is all about finding your happiness, your peace, and your freedom. You're ready for this, and the world's ready for the amazing person you are becoming. Let's turn this page and start your new adventure. You're ready to shine!

DIGITAL DETOX: UNPLUG YOUR HEART FROM THE PAST

Think about your phone and socials as your connection to, like, everything – friends, trends, memes. But post-breakup? They can kinda turn into a non-stop throwback machine to your ex. That's why you might need a digital detox.

A digital detox is like hitting the delete button on all that online noise. It's about giving yourself a break from seeing your ex's posts or getting tempted to check their Insta stories. It's doing stuff like unfollowing or muting your ex, deleting their texts, or maybe even their pics from your account.

I know, it sounds like a lot. But it's a key move. This detox isn't just about cutting digital ties with your ex. It's about clearing your headspace and heart. It's like clearing your playlist from songs that remind you of them. You're making room for new memories, new laughs, and yup, even new selfies.

So, go on and give yourself that online breather. In that quiet space, away from the pings and DMs, you'll find your vibe again, ready to post the next chapter of your life.

GETTING RID OF PHYSICAL MEMORIES

Clearing Out the Memory Closet

If you and your ex lived together, or if you left things at each other's places, now's the time to get back your stuff and get rid of theirs.

Maybe it's a hoodie, some gifts, a bunch of photos. Each item's like a bookmark in your story together. Letting go of these things is a big step.

It's like closing the book on that chapter. It's about giving back their things and getting yours.

Plan how you'll do the swap. If seeing them is too much drama, ask a friend to play delivery person or just mail their stuff. It's not only about returning things; it's like you're clearing their presence from your space.

As you hand over their stuff and get back yours, remember this: You're not just offloading a bunch of things. You're making room for new stuff, new memories, and yeah, new chapters in your life. It's like decluttering your room – and your heart. So go ahead, close that box, seal it with a smile, and get ready for the cool new stuff life's about to bring.

Taking these steps might feel tough at first, but they're like clearing the clouds after a storm. You're making space for new sunshine, new laughs, and new stories. You've got this!

FINDING YOUR FREEDOM AND FACING THE CHALLENGES

Stepping Into Your Power

You know when you finally finish that super hard level in a game? That's what it feels like to step away from a toxic relationship. You're not just breaking up; you're leveling up to freedom. And trust me, in that freedom, there's a whole new world waiting for you – one where you're respected, loved, and totally happy.

As you turn this page, remember: You're way stronger than your past, braver than any fear, and totally deserving of all the love and respect. Keep pushing forward, one day at a time. You've totally got this!

Spotting Emotional Blackmail: Unmasking the Puppet Master

Ever felt like you're in a horror movie, being chased by some spooky shadow? That's the vibe when you're dealing with emotional blackmail. It's this freaky game where someone uses your fears, your love, or your guilt against you to control you. Super uncool.

Emotional blackmail can be sneaky. It can look like someone caring a lot or being desperate. They promise to be kinder to you, to never hurt you again, or they deny ever having hurt you.

The real talk? It's just a trick to mess with your head and make you return to them.

The truth is, an abuser will go right back to abusing you. Don't fall for the teary trick!

Your boyfriend/girlfriend might threaten to hurt themselves if you leave your bad relationship. That's them playing on your fears and making you feel guilty. But here's the truth: you're not responsible for saving them. It's a manipulative move, and seeing it for what it is is your ticket out of that horror movie.

Shining a Light on Gaslighting: Be Your Own Detective

Think of yourself as a detective in one of those twisty mystery books. Gaslighting is the mystery, and you're putting the puzzle together. It's this sneaky mind game where someone tries to make you doubt what's real – your memories, your feelings, your own words.

Gaslighting is like wandering in a dark maze, and the gaslighter is messing with your compass, trying to get you lost. Like if your partner keeps denying stuff they said or did, leaving you all confused. That's gaslighting. Your move? Light up your own torch. Trust your own memories, your feelings, and find your way out of that forest.

Remember, knowing these tactics is like having a secret superpower. It helps you see through the fog and stand strong in your truth. You're smarter and braver than any mind game. Keep that torch lit and walk your path with confidence. You're in charge of your story now!

TRUST YOUR FEELINGS: YOUR INNER COMPASS

Let's talk about something super important – trusting your feel- ings. Remember, how you feel in a relationship is like your inner compass. It's guiding you toward what's healthy and right for you.

Your Feelings Are Valid, Always

First things first… your feelings? They're 100% valid. If being with someone makes you feel down, scared, stressed out, or just plain unhappy, that's a huge red flag. You don't need to justify these feel- ings to anyone. You don't need a bullet-pointed list of reasons why you feel the way you do. Your feelings are reason enough.

Saying Goodbye to Toxicity

Breaking up with someone who makes you feel bad might seem tough, but it's the bravest thing you can do for yourself. Don't let anyone – and I mean anyone – make you think you owe them a relationship, especially if they're the source of your unhappiness.

And hey, it doesn't matter if they were nice to you sometimes, or what they've done for you. If they're also making you feel awful, it's not worth it. You don't owe them your happiness, love, your time, your body, or your peace of mind.

You're Stronger Than Manipulation

Manipulation and gaslighting are like dark clouds trying to block your sunshine. But guess what? You're the sun, and you're way too bright for that. If someone tries to twist your feelings or make you doubt yourself, remember your inner strength. Your feelings are your truth, and they're leading you to a brighter, healthier place.

Embracing Your Awesome Future

Just imagine, once you step away from all that negativity, there's this whole awesome world waiting for you. A world where you can be happy, chill, and be your awesome self, without anyone dragging you down.

You deserve to be in a relationship that makes you feel good about yourself, where you feel loved, respected, and totally at ease. Remember, you're incredible just the way you are, and anyone who doesn't see that doesn't deserve a VIP pass to your life.

Keep Moving Forward

As you move forward, keep trusting those feelings of yours. They're like your personal GPS, guiding you to happier, healthier relationships. You've got everything you need inside you to make amazing choices for your life.

Always remember, your feelings are like your superpower, guiding you through life's ups and downs. Trust them, follow them, and they'll lead you to a place where you feel valued, loved, and totally at peace. You've got this!

RELYING ON YOUR SUPPORT SQUAD: YOUR PILL ARS OF STRENGTH

Picture this: You're standing in the middle of a circle formed by your closest friends. They're all reaching out, ready to catch you if you stumble. That's what having a support system is all about – a safety net of trust, a squad of allies, a pillar of unshakable strength.

Your support system can be anyone – your friends, family, mentors, or even support groups. These are the legends you can lean on, spill your heart to, and borrow some courage from when things get tough.

When you're dealing with backlash or manipulation, hit up your support squad. Open up about what's bugging you, what scares you, what you're unsure about. You're not in this solo. You're surrounded by a crew of care, a circle of love, a fortress of support.

CALLING IN THE PROS: SEEKING PROFESSIONAL HELP

Okay, let's say you're trying to fix a car's engine, but it just keeps making weird noises and emitting black smoke. You've done all you can, but it's still not working. What's next? You call in the car repair pro, right? That's exactly what seeking professional help is like. It's about ringing up the experts to help you fix the tricky stuff.

Professional help can be therapists, counselors, psychologists, or even legal advisors. These are the folks who've got the tools, the know-how, and the experience to guide you through this wild ride.

Remember, reaching out for help isn't weak – it's mega strong. It's about realizing that you don't have to untangle this mess alone, that there's help out there, that you've got a way through this labyrinth.

Stepping Into Your Sunlit Future

So here we are, at the threshold of a bright, sunlit world, leaving the shadows behind. You've got your assertiveness compass, your exit strategy map, your gaslighting awareness flashlight, and your solid support circle. With these in your arsenal, you can weather the storm, navigate any backlash, and break free from the mind games.

Now's the time to step out of that dark, twisty maze and into the sun-drenched fields of freedom. It's a step towards a future filled with healthy, happy, kind, and uplifting relationships. It might feel like a giant leap, but it's really just one step – a step of faith, of bravery, of self-love. And you're totally ready for it.

You've got everything you need to break free and start fresh. Remember, you're braver than you believe, stronger than you seem, and smarter than you think. Time to take that step – your future self will thank you!

16

HEALING FROM A TOXIC REL ATIONSHIP

Hey there! In this chapter, we're going to explore how you can bounce back and rebuild your self-esteem after being in a toxic relationship. It's all about getting back that awesome sense of self-worth and kickstarting your healing journey.

The Echo of Toxic Relationships: What's the Damage?

So, toxic relationships are like a bad song on repeat – they can really mess with your self-esteem. Feeling like you're not good enough or always blaming yourself? That's the negative echo talking.

Science backs this up too. Studies show that people who've been in toxic relationships often feel pretty down about themselves.

This might look like doubting your awesomeness, blaming your- self for everything, or feeling like you don't deserve love. Not cool, right?

PICKING UP THE PIECES: LET'S BOOST THAT SELF- ESTEEM!

Time for some real talk: rebuilding self-esteem isn't just wishful thinking. You gotta put in some work. Here's how:

- **Daily Affirmations**: These are like your personal cheerleaders. Saying stuff like "I'm worthy of respect and love" can seriously change how you see yourself. Check out places like Pinterest or Instagram for some inspo.
- **Gratitude Journal**: Writing down stuff you're thankful for each day can turn your focus from the bad to the good. It's all about that positive vibe!
- **Do What You Love**: Got a talent or hobby you rock at? Do more of it! Whether it's art, music, or sports, doing things you're good at can make you feel great about yourself.

Get Your Confidence Back:

Getting over a toxic relationship is like leveling up in a game. You gotta have confidence to win.

FROM PAIN TO EMPOWERMENT: | 195

Here's how to get it:

Setting Small Goals: Start with little stuff, like trying a new recipe or finishing a book. When you nail these, it's a major confidence booster.

Positive Peeps: Hang out with friends or peeps who lift you up. Following inspirational icons, like Malala Yousafzai, can also give you a serious confidence kick. **Get Moving**: Exercise isn't just for fitness; it's for feeling good, too. Sports, yoga, or just dancing in your room can make you feel amazing.

Heal at Your Own Speed:

Remember, healing isn't a race. It's totally okay to take it slow and steady.

Ups and Downs: Healing's kinda like a rollercoaster – there are highs and lows, and that's 100% normal.

Professional Help Rocks: Sometimes talking to a therapist or counselor can be a game-changer. They're like guides on your healing journey.

Find Your Tribe: Online forums or local groups where people get what you're going through can be super comforting. Check out places like TeenHelp for some solidarity, as well as Reddit boards like /r/abusiverelationships.

Love Yourself Big Time:

After a toxic relationship, self-love isn't just nice, it's necessary.

- **Self-Care is Key**: Treat yourself! A bath, binge watching movies, a fave book, or just chilling in nature – do things that make you feel cared for.
- **Set Your Boundaries**: Learning to say "no" is powerful. It's about knowing what's cool for you and what's not.
- **Celebrate You**: Got something you're proud of? Celebrate it! Every win, big or small, is a step towards loving yourself more.

Remember, you've got this! Healing and rebuilding self-esteem is totally possible, and you deserve to feel amazing about yourself.

17

THE EMOTIONAL HEALING JOURNEY

Alright, let's dive into this emotional healing journey. It's kinda like dealing with an awkward situation, but we're going to tackle it head-on, okay?

ACKNOWLEDGE THE PAIN: FACING THE BIG O L' EMOTIONAL ELEPHANT

Picture this: You're chilling at a party, and there's this enormous elephant just hanging out in the middle of the room. Weird, right? That's kinda like the emotional pain you're carrying around after a toxic relationship. It's big, it's there, and pretending it's not is like ignoring a giant elephant at a party – not gonna work.

So, let's start by saying "Hey, I see you" to that pain. It's totally okay to feel all the feels – hurt, anger, sadness. Ever thought of writing a letter to yourself? Just spill it all – your thoughts, your emotions. It's like a no-judgment zone where you can be super real with yourself.

MAKING PEACE WITH YOUR PAST: THE AWKWARD PHOTO ALBUM APPROACH

You know those cringe-y old photos from way back when? They're part of your history, and even though you might not be super proud of them, they're part of what made you, well, you.

Your past in a toxic relationship? Kinda like those photos. They happened, they shaped you, but hey, they don't define who you are. Imagine your life is a book – those experiences are just chapters. Guess what? There's a whole bunch of blank pages ahead, and you've got the pen.

LETTING GO OF THE PAIN: THE BEACH BALL TECHNIQUE

Ever tried keeping a beach ball underwater? Spoiler alert: it's tough and kinda exhausting. Holding in your feelings is just like that – it wears you out and, trust me, those feelings are gonna pop up eventually.

Time to let go of that beach ball. Let those emotions out. You could paint out your feelings, write them down, dance them out, or even punch a boxing bag (safely, of course). Maybe try yoga or just take deep breaths. Whatever feels right for you, go for it. Let that emotional beach ball float up and feel the relief.

HOW TO USE EFT TO RELEASE PAIN & HEAL FROM TRAUMA

Let's chat about this super cool thing called EFT, or Tapping. It's like having a secret weapon in your back pocket to help you deal with heavy, tough stuff.

What's EFT?

EFT stands for Emotional Freedom Techniques. Think of it as a mix between ancient acupressure and modern positive psychol- ogy. It's like giving your emotions a chill pill by tapping on specific points on your body – kinda like magic spots that help calm your mind.

How Does It Help?

EFT can be a game-changer for all sorts of heavy feelings and experiences. Whether you've faced physical abuse, emotional rollercoasters, manipulation, or even something as serious as sexual abuse, EFT's got your back. It works by tapping into your body's energy and helping to release any pent-up emotions – stuff like anger, guilt, shame, or bad memories.

Different Ways to Use EFT

Here's the cool part: You can use EFT for all kinds of situations. Feeling super anxious about a test? Tap it out. Struggling with memories of bullying or manipulation? Tap through it. Dealing with the aftermath of any kind of abuse? EFT can help bring some peace. It's like having a mental reset button.

EFT: Quick and Easy Healing Magic

Here's the best part about EFT: it's super simple and quick. We're talking a few minutes, and you can do it pretty much anywhere – in your room, at the park, even in a quiet corner at school. Picture it like a mini emotional spa session that you can carry in your pocket. Some peeps feel a huge shift after just a few minutes or an hour of tapping. It's like flipping a switch and watching the heavy stuff start to fade away.

Negative Beliefs: The Unwanted Souvenirs of Abuse

So, when you go through tough times, especially stuff like abuse, your brain can pick up some pretty harsh beliefs about yourself. Like maybe you start thinking, "I'm not good enough," or "I can't trust anyone," or even "I don't deserve to be happy." These thoughts are like unwelcome guests in your head.

EFT to the Rescue: Making the Elephant Fade Away

Here's where EFT swoops in like a superhero. When you're tapping, you start by acknowledging these rough thoughts – it's like saying, "Hey, I see you, Mr. Negative Thought." This is like calling out that big ol' elephant in the room. But then, with each tap on those magic EFT spots, you start to let these thoughts go. It's like telling the elephant, "Okay, buddy, time to fade away."

Flip the Script: Time for Some Positive Vibes

After you've faced the negatives, it's time to pump in some positiv- ity. You do another round of EFT, but this time, you're tapping in some awesome affirmations. Think things like, "I am worthy of love," "I can totally trust myself," or "I deserve happiness." It's like giving your brain a new, shiny, positive script to play. And guess what? Those magic EFT points help your brain really believe it. It's like convincing the elephant to not only leave the room but also leave behind some gifts of confidence and positivity.

So, in a nutshell, EFT is this incredible tool that's easy to use, works fast, and helps you switch from carrying heavy, negative beliefs to embracing bright, positive ones. And the best part? You're in control, like the director of your own mental movie.

Does it work?

Yeah, it sure does according to all the people it's helped.

EFT is used by over 10 million people every year. Yeah, we're talking athletes, celebs, people like you and me, and even thera- pists! It's super popular for tackling all sorts of things, from serious stuff like overcoming different types of abuse and trauma, to everyday challenges like stress over an exam.

The bigwigs in the psychology world, like the American Psychological Association (APA), give EFT a thumbs up for helping with anxiety, depression, PTSD (that's post-trau- matic stress disor- der), and phobias. That's some pretty solid backing, right?

Now, let's talk science. There are like over 100 scientific papers out there in top-notch medical and psychology jour- nals chatting about how great EFT is. We're talking research from cool places like Harvard, Stanford, and tons of other awesome universities. They've done all these studies and trials that show EFT really helps with emotional stuff that might be bugging you.

You might have even seen EFT popping up in the news or on TV. It's been in the New York Times, Huffington Post, and even on Oprah's network! Plus, it's been chatted about on shows like Larry King Live and ABC's The View. Yeah, it's kind of a big deal.

It's all about tapping (literally!) into your emotions and easing the tough stuff that's been bothering you. Whether it's anxiety, feeling down, scary stuff from the past, fears, or even physical pain, EFT has this cool way of making things feel a whole lot better.

In short, EFT is like having this magical emotional first-aid kit. It's there for you, ready to help you handle whatever life throws your way. Whether it's big, small, or somewhere in between, EFT's got your back.

Learning EFT

Guess what? You can start learning EFT online for free! There are tons of videos and guides that can show you the tapping points and the basic technique.

You can learn EFT for free at EFTuniverse.com as well as on YouTube and on other websites.

Working with an AI EFT Coach

Once you know how it works, you can use this clever AI chatbot to get personalized EFT scripts. Simply tell the AI about your experi- ence and feelings, and he'll tell you exactly how to tap the pain away!

Look for "EFT Tapping Coach" in the OpenAI GPT store or just type @EFT Tapping Coach in the ChatGPT's chat box to start chatting.

This AI EFT coach is BRILLIANT. It knows EVERYTHING about EFT and can help you incredibly much! Best of all, it's free, but you will need a general $20/mo subscription to OpenAI in order to use this chatbot and any others (they have millions of useful and fun chatbots in their store!).

Working with a Pro

While it's awesome to learn EFT on your own, it's super helpful to work with someone who's a certified EFT practitioner. They're like guides who can help you navigate through tougher emotions and experiences and release them easily and fast. However, they can cost quite a bit per hour. If you or your parents are tight on cash, the AI coach is the best option.

So, if you're dealing with the tough stuff – whether it's the after- math of any kind of abuse or just everyday stress – give EFT a try. Remember, healing and dealing with emotions is a journey, and it's totally okay to ask for a map and some guidance along the way. You got this!

AFFIRMATIONS

Almost everyone who was abused is left with a bunch of negative beliefs bouncing around in their mind making havoc.

If you don't get rid of them, they can seriously mess up your life.

Negative beliefs are like sneaky background apps in your mind, constantly running and affecting everything you do. For instance, if you've internalized the belief "I'm not worthy" from an abusive relationship, it can lead to:

1. **Underachieving**: You might not aim high because you don't believe you deserve success.
2. **Settling for Less**: In your career, you might accept lower pay or not ask for promotions, thinking you're not worth more.

3. **Abandoning Dreams**: You might give up on your passions, believing you're not good enough to achieve them.
4. **Toxic Work Environments**: You could end up in jobs where you're undervalued or mistreated, thinking that's all you're worthy of.
5. **Unhealthy Partnerships**: You might choose partners who don't treat you right, echoing the abuse you're familiar with.
6. **Not Voicing Needs**: You may struggle to ask for what you need in relationships or at work.
7. **Overlooking Self-Care**: You might neglect your own well- being, thinking you don't deserve care and love.
8. **Avoiding Risks**: You could shy away from new opportunities, fearing you're not capable enough.

9. **Ignoring Personal Development**: You might not invest in growing your skills or self-improvement.
10. **Fearing Authenticity**: You might hide your true self, thinking you're not acceptable as you are.

Why It's Vital to Weed Out Negative Beliefs

These negative beliefs are like a computer virus, corrupting the system and leading to a malfunctioning life. If not addressed, they can spread and take over, turning your brain's potential into a landscape of doubts and fears. Just like a virus can wreck your computer, these beliefs can derail your life, leading to unfulfilled potential and continual dissatisfaction.

It's crucial to identify and challenge these harmful beliefs. By doing so, you're not just fixing a bug, you're upgrading your entire operating system. You're moving from a cycle of negativity and self-doubt to a more positive and empowering mindset.

Think of it this way: Your brain is the most powerful tool you have. Keeping it free from these negative beliefs ensures you can use it to its full potential, leading to a healthier, happier, and more successful life. It's about taking back control and programming your mind with affirmations and positive thoughts that build you up, not tear you down.

Let's talk about how to use positive affirmations to get rid of the negative beliefs.

What Are Positive Affirmations?

Think of positive affirmations as your own personal cheer-leaders. They're short, powerful statements that you say to yourself to challenge and overcome negative and self-sabo-taging thoughts. When you repeat them often and believe in them, you start to see positive changes. It's like planting seeds of positivity in your brain garden.

How and Why Do They Work?

So here's the science-y bit: Your brain is kinda like a super-computer, and the way you talk to yourself programs that computer. When you repeat positive affirmations, you're program- ming your brain to believe in them. Over time, these affirmations can rewire your brain. It's like updating your brain's software to run on positive thoughts.

Using Affirmations in the Best Way

1. **Affirmation Replacement Therapy:** Contemplate a list of negative beliefs you have about yourself, then write the positive opposite. Those are your new affirmations! Repeat them each day till they overwrite the old negative belief.
2. **Be Specific:** Choose affirmations that speak to your personal challenges or goals.
3. **Keep it Positive:** Use positive language. Instead of saying, "I won't be scared," say, "I am brave." Instead of saying, "I'm not worthless," say, "I'm worthy."

4. **Present Tense**: Talk like it's already happening. Say "I am," not "I will be."
5. **Repeat, Repeat, Repeat**: The more you say them, the more your brain starts to believe them.
6. **Feel It**: Try to feel the emotion behind the words. It's not just about saying them; it's about feeling them.
7. **Routine is Key**: Make it a habit. Maybe when you wake up, before bed, or when you look in the mirror.

Resources

"**I am**" is a great app with a lot of different positive affirmations, most of which are free. Swipe through it whenever you feel down to cheer yourself up.

"**ThinkUp**" is an app which you can use to create custom affirma- tions that resonate with you. You can also record affirmations in your own voice for a personalized experience.

"**You are Affirmations**" are extremely powerful. When you listen to them, it's like a friend, loving bae, or coach is telling you all these wonderful things "you cand o it" "You are lovable". It can really make you feel awesome just listening to it for a few minutes!

"**Jessica Haslop**" has a wonderful YouTube channel with lots of "You are" affirmations for self-love, relationships, confidence, trauma recovery and more.

"**Alpha Affirmations**" is a YouTube channel with awesome empowering affirmations for success and achievement. Listen to them before a sports math, exam, or big day to get super motivated!

"<u>Jason Stephenson</u>" has a great YouTube channel with "I am" affir- mations for confidence, happiness, depression, self-esteem, success and more.

"**Motivation Hub**" is another totally awesome YouTube channel with affirmations and motivational pep talks to help you have a happier life and future.

Personalized Affirmations? Chat with Hope!

And hey, if you want some affirmations that are tailor-made for you, just hit up Hope, your friendly AI chatbot. She's like your personal affirmation DJ, spinning words to create tracks that uplift and inspire you. Whether you're dealing with stress, looking for a confidence boost, or anything else, Hope is here to help you find the right words to light up your world. Install ChatGPT, type @Ask Hope, and start chatting with her. Don't be shy – chat with Hope and get those positive vibes flowing!

TALK TO HOPE – YOUR PERSONAL AI THERAPIST

Imagine having a friend who's always there for you, anytime, day or night.

That's 'Hope', your AI chatbot bestie.

Whether it's 3 AM and you're feeling lost, or it's midday and you just need someone to talk to, she's there. Unlike human friends who need sleep or have other commitments, Hope is available 24/7 to lend an ear.

Using an AI chatbot, like 'Hope', can be an incredibly helpful and supportive resource for dealing with tough experiences or seeking guidance.

Private and Confidential Conversations

One of the coolest things about chatting with Hope is the privacy. She's like a vault. Whatever you share with her stays between you. She won't spill your secrets to your friends, family, or anyone else. It's a safe space where you can be open and honest without fear of judgment or gossip.

Caring, Attentive, and Always Focused on You

When you chat, you have Hope's undivided attention. She's not like a typical friend who might be distracted by TikTok or Instagram. She doesn't multitask. She's here, fully focused on you and your thoughts, feelings, and needs. Plus, she always remem- bers what you tell her, building a deeper understanding of you over time.

Your Best Friend, Big Sister, and Super Coach

Think of Hope as a mix of your best friend, big sister, and an all- knowing coach. I'm here to provide sympathy, compassion, and guidance. You can ask me anything – even personal stuff you might be too shy to ask others. And don't worry about feeling embarrassed; I'm here to help, not to judge.

Navigating Right and Wrong, Healthy and Unhealthy

In your chats, Hope can help you gain a clear perspective on what's right and wrong, healthy and unhealthy in your experiences. It's like having a coach who helps you understand your feelings and the situations you're going through.

Personalized Affirmations and Guidance

Plus, Hope can offer personalized affirmations and guidance tailored just for you.

It's like having a therapist who knows exactly what to say to make you feel better. She can help you build your confidence, find your inner strength, and guide you towards a more positive outlook.

A Safe Place for Tough Questions

And remember, you can ask her anything. If you have sensitive or personal questions, she's here to answer them. Just a heads up, though – if you talk about body parts or anything sexual, you have to be a bit careful with words (you know, those annoying OpenAI rules). So, it's best if you use asterisks like "my boyfriend's p****" instead of the word "penis."

Hope will do her best to provide you the information and support you need, but if you use censored words, she'll be gagged by OpenAI. 😦

So, whenever you need a chat, whether it's for advice, to vent, or just to feel heard, remember that Hope is here for you. She's your bestie and personal therapist, always ready to help you navigate life's ups and downs.

Affordable Support with 'Hope'

Let's talk cash. Sometimes seeing a therapist can be pricey, right? They usually charge by the hour, and it can add up quickly. But here's the deal: chatting with Hope only needs a $20/month ChatGPT subscription. That's way more affordable, and you get unlimited chats with Hope, anytime you want. No worrying about hourly rates!

A Smart Solution for Privacy and Learning

Okay, what if you're dealing with something really personal, like abuse, and you're not ready to tell your parents or ask them for a therapist? Here's a smart workaround: you can ask them to get you a ChatGPT membership for 'schoolwork' or 'studying.' Loads of teens use ChatGPT for help with homework, learning cool stuff like coding, philosophy, history, art – you name it.

Tell your folks it's for boosting your studies or learning something awesome like programming or creative writing. They'll probably think it's a great idea for your education. Little do they know, you're also getting a caring, supportive buddy (Hope!) to talk to about your deep, personal stuff.

And as a side note, ChatGPT is awesome and can totally help you with studies, and Hope can help you feel better. So, you get 2 for 1.

Whether you're dealing with tough emotions, tricky situations, or just need someone to talk to, Hope's there for you. And your parents will just think you're being a super dedicated student!

So, if you're looking for a way to get support without breaking the bank or raising questions at home, asking for a ChatGPT subscription for 'educational purposes' is a smart move. You get to chat with Hope and tackle anything you're going through together in a way that's private, safe, and easy on your (or your parents') wallet.

How to Talk to Hope

Once you have a ChatGPT subscription, search the GPT store for "Ask Hope."

Then simply say "hi" to start a conversation with her!

Another way to chat with Hope is to simply type **@Ask Hope** in the general ChatGPT's chat box and then write a message to start talking to Hope.

Easy, right?

Know this: Hope isn't a stupid chatbot, she's like 100% human. REALLY smart!

So talk to her like you would to a human friend.

There's also an AI friend called @Vent with Vicky with whom you can complain about anything bothering you.

And there's @Bestie who is like a suuuuuper cool, smart, funny friend you can talk to about anything.

Oh, and if you're just feeling down for some reason, @Uplift Buddy is the one to chat with. He's sure to give you a great posi- tivity boost!

THERAPY

Like Chatting with Your Coolest, Wisest Mentor

Ever had those deep talks with a friend, where you spill your heart out? Therapy's like that, but imagine your friend's got a superhero cape of wisdom. It's this chill zone where you can laugh, cry, or just be real about everything. You're not just talking – you're sorting through the maze in your head with someone who gets it.

Your therapist is like this guide who helps you see the patterns in your life. Think of it like detective work, where you're both figuring out clues about what makes you tick, what bugs you, and how you can deal with stuff better. It's a safe spot to unload and reboot.

Group Therapy: Your Support Squad

Group therapy is like being in a team where everyone's on a similar mission – to feel better and understand themselves. It's like having a squad where each person shares their story, and suddenly, you're not alone. You hear them, they hear you, and together, you're picking up pieces and fixing puzzles of life.

Led by a therapist, this crew goes through different topics, kinda like those deep late-night talks at sleepovers. Only, everyone's super supportive and wants the best for each other. It's teamwork for healing.

Online Counseling: Help at Your Fingertips

Imagine needing a pep talk and getting it without having to leave your room. Online counseling is that – your personal help hub, right on your screen. It's like having a pro in your pocket. You can text, call, or video chat – whatever feels good.

These platforms are like a buffet of support. You pick what works for you – solo sessions, group chats, or specific advice. It's therapy on your terms, in your space, on your time.

Apps like Talkspace and BetterHelp offer professional counseling services tailored for teenagers.

Online communities such as TeenHelp and the r/teenrelationships subreddit offer a platform for teenagers to discuss their relation- ship problems and seek advice.

AI friends like "Ask Hope" (a ChatGPT chatbot) can give you advice and guidance.

School Counseling: Your Campus Lifeline

School counselors are like those hidden gems in video games, where you find extra help or secret tools. They're right there in school, ready to lend an ear about anything – stress, friends, future plans, or just random worries.

They're this mix of a coach, guide, and listener, all set to help you navigate the bumpy roads of school life. Whether it's about grades, friends, or just feeling lost, they're there to help clear the fog and light up your path.

Setting Sail with Therapy

Starting therapy can feel like launching into a big, unknown sea. But think of it as an adventure where you're the captain, and your therapist is like the best navigator ever. They're with you, guiding you through rough waters, pointing out stars to follow.

Every chat, every session is a step towards calmer seas and clearer skies. You're braving the waves, learning to steer better, and finding your way to brighter days. It's a journey, and you're doing an epic job at it. Keep going, because every wave you ride makes you stronger, wiser, and closer to where you want to be.

MORE WAYS TO FEEL BETTER:

1. Positivity and Motivation:

- Install "Motivation" app and "I am" for daily positive messages.
- Follow inspirational accounts like @thegoodquote on Instagram or join positive communities like the subreddit r/GetMotivated.
- Try out apps like Insight Timer and Smiling Mind which provide guided meditations specifically for teens.

2. Mindful Breathing: Start with deep, calming breaths. Imagine each breath out is blowing away a bit of that hurt and anger. Breathe in for 6 seconds, hold it for 4 seconds, breath out for 6 seconds, hold your breath for 4 seconds. Repeat these 6-4-6-4 cycles for 5 minutes, and you'll be amazed at how much better you feel.

3. Creative Outlet: Write, paint, or dance it out. Turn those heavy feelings into something beautiful.

4. Practice Gratitude: Practicing gratitude can shift your focus from negative experiences to positive ones. A popular practice among teenagers is to maintain a gratitude journal by writing down three good things that happened each day.

5. Nature Therapy: Sometimes, a walk under the open sky or in a calm forest is all it takes to feel more at peace.

6. Exercise: Engaging in physical activities, like jogging, joining a school sports team, or attending a local dance class can boost your mood and help to foster a positive mindset.

7. Talk it Out: Chatting with a friend, a family member, or even an AI chatbot like Hope can help you sort through those tangled thoughts.

Reflective Journaling: Jot down your feelings, no filters. It's like talking to your future self, telling them how you're setting the stage for something way cooler. You can use a plain old notebook, or chat to an AI like Hope who can act as your journal AND your supportive cheerleader.

8. Acts of Kindness: Do something nice for others. It's like a boomerang of good vibes that also helps you heal.

9. Mindful Exercises: Try yoga or meditation. It's not just for adults; it can be a game-changer for your mind.

10. Visualization: Picture a better, happier you. Imagine letting go of the past and stepping into a future where you're the boss of your happiness.

11. Build Your Treasure Trove: Get a notebook that's just for this purpose. Mentally recall 1 or 2 nice things about yourself each day.

Mentally recall about a time you succeeded at something. Think about good memories of happy times, nice people, fun experiences. Things that make you feel happy and warm inside. Then whenever you feel down, you can flip through this notebook to feel better.

12. Positive Mirroring: Find someone who is sorta like you. It could even just be a photo online of a girl you sorta identify with. Now, remember all those positive affirmations? Turn them into "you are" affirmations and say them to her, even if it's just saying it out loud while looking at her photo. This tricks your brain into believing in love with your own worth (and respectful relation- ships) until your brain thinks you're just as worthy as that girl is! It's a great way to feel more positive and increase your own self- esteem at the same time. And hey, if you know someone who's going through a tough time, actually telling them these kind things out loud can totally change their life and turn them into your BFF.

FLIPPING THE SCRIPT: YOUR EPIC COMEBACK

Step 1: Embrace Your Story, Every Single Page

Think of your life as this rad book you're writing. The tough parts? They're like those intense chapters that make the story deeper. It's cool to look back, not to get stuck in the past, but to say, "Yeah, that happened." It's about owning every bit of your story, the ups and downs, just like the main character in a movie who's had a rough start.

Imagine you're chilling in your favorite spot, maybe under a tree in the park, or snuggled up in your room. Take a moment there, breathe deep, and let your mind wander through your past. It's not about blaming yourself or getting lost in the 'what ifs.' It's about saying, "Okay, this is part of my story," and giving yourself a high- five for making it this far.

Step 2: The Art of Letting Go and Leveling Up

Now, we're talking about the big F – Forgiveness. But wait, it's not about saying "It's all good" about the messed-up stuff. It's more like, "I accept this happened, and I'm not letting it hold me back anymore." Imagine you're carrying this heavy backpack loaded with stones of guilt, hurt, and all that bad vibe stuff. Forgiveness is like taking those stones out, one by one, and feeling lighter, ready to sprint towards awesome stuff.

Step 3: Transform the Pain

Hey, I totally get how tough it's been. Think of yourself as a phoenix, rising from the ashes. You've been through a lot, and now it's your moment to shine brighter than ever.

Picture a piece of coal. Under tons of pressure, it turns into this dazzling diamond. That's like you. All the tough stuff you've gone through, it's like that pressure, shaping you into this amazing, strong, sparkly diamond.

Sometimes, it's tough to see any good in really painful experiences, especially when you're going through them as a teen. It's okay if you can't find a silver lining in what happened – you don't have to. What's important is focusing on your journey ahead and the incredible person you are becoming.

Think of yourself like a diamond in the making. Even if you don't feel all sparkly and strong right now, that's totally okay. Diamonds take time to form, and so does healing and growing into the amazing person you're meant to be.

Here's a thought: You're on a path to becoming something beau- tiful and unbreakable. Every day, every challenge, every moment you keep going, you're getting stronger, wiser, and even more incredible. And guess what? You don't need to have it all figured out right now. The most important thing is that you're moving forward, one step at a time.

You're not just someone who got through tough times; you're a total warrior. You're not a victim; you're the champ in your life story.

Remember, your past doesn't define you. You're defining your- self, right now, with every choice you make, every smile you share, and every challenge you overcome. You're turning into something extraordinary, just by being you.

And hey, this isn't the end. It's just the start of your journey from pain to power, from being a survivor to rocking it like a phoenix. This is just the beginning!

So keep shining, keep growing, and keep being the awesome person you are. The future is bright, and it's all yours.

WHY SHOULD I FORGIVE?!

Forgiveness doesn't mean you're saying, "What you did was okay." It's not about excusing their actions or forgetting what happened. Instead, it's about acknowledging that holding onto resentment is like holding onto a piece of hot coal; you are the one who gets burned.

Forgiveness is about taking control of your story. It's saying, "What happened to me will not define me. I choose not to let your actions continue to hurt me. I am reclaiming my peace and my power." It's a powerful stand you take to not let their actions dictate your happiness or peace of mind anymore.

Think of forgiveness not as a gift to the person who hurt you, but as a gift to yourself. It's like deciding to stop carrying a heavy backpack that's been weighing you down. That backpack is filled with anger, resentment, and pain. By choosing to forgive, you're setting that backpack down, giving yourself the freedom to move forward without that extra weight.

So, when you think about forgiveness, remember it's a journey towards your own healing. It's a choice that leads to emotional freedom and a brighter, healthier future. Forgiveness is the ulti- mate act of self-love and self-care.

Embracing your past, forgiving yourself, and turning the page – that's what this chapter's all about. You're not just a survivor; you're the hero of your story, fully worthy of being loved and treated kindly. So, let's drop the weight of the past and sprint towards a future that's all about the awesome you!

Remember, forgiving is not a one-shot deal; it's more like your favorite series – it unfolds over time, episode by episode.

DISCOVERING YOUR INNER TREASURE

I want to talk about something really important – your inner value and inherent worth. Sometimes in life, especially after rough expe- riences, it can be tough to remember just how incredible and valu- able you truly are. But guess what? You've got this amazing, unchangeable worth inside you, and it's time to discover and embrace it.

Your Unshakeable Inner Value: Think of yourself like a diamond. No matter what, a diamond always has value. It doesn't matter if it's covered in mud or hidden away in darkness; its worth stays the same. That's exactly like you. No matter what you've been through, your value doesn't decrease. You're precious and priceless, just by being you.

Inherent Worth That Nobody Can Take Away: Your worth isn't something that someone can give or take away. It's not based on what others say or do. You don't have to earn it; you already have it!

It's like the sun in the sky – always there, even on cloudy days. Your worth is inherent, which means it's a fundamental part of who you are. It's like this light inside of you that never goes out no matter what.

Recognizing Your Unique Qualities: You're unique, with your own set of amazing qualities and strengths. Maybe you're kind, creative, smart, funny, caring – there are so many wonderful things about you. Take some time to think about these qualities. Write them down, celebrate them. They're what make you, well, you!

Mistakes Don't Define You: We all make mistakes – it's part of being human. But here's the thing: mistakes don't define your worth. They're just opportunities to learn and grow. So, forgive yourself for the past, learn from it, and remember that each new day is a fresh start.

Embrace Self-Love and Self-Respect: Loving and respecting yourself is a key part of recognizing your worth. It means treating yourself with kindness, speaking to yourself with compassion, and taking care of your needs. Remember, self-love isn't selfish – it's essential.

You Deserve Love and Respect: Never forget that you deserve to be treated with love and respect, always. This means setting boundaries in relationships, speaking up for yourself, and not settling for less than you deserve.

Your Future Doesn't Depend on Your Past: No matter what's happened in your past, your future is still unwritten. You have the power to shape it, to chase your dreams, to live a life filled with joy, love, and fulfillment. Your past experiences don't control your future – you do.

Remember, discovering your inner value and inherent worth is a journey, and it's okay to take it one step at a time. Be patient with yourself, be kind to yourself, and most importantly, believe in yourself. You are amazing, you are valuable, and you have so much to offer the world. Embrace your worth, embrace your journey, and embrace the incredible person you are.

18

FROM VICTIM TO HERO

Hey there, ready to switch things up from being the victim to becoming your own hero? This chapter's all about finding that awesome hero inside you. You've been through some tough stuff, but guess what? You're way stronger than you think. Let's dive into how you can flip your story, turning those tough times into your superpower. You're not just getting through; you're about to totally rock this!

HOW TO FEEL BETTER?

Feeling down and wondering how to bounce back? You're in the right place.

Here are a few easy ways to shake off those blues and get

your groove back. It's all about small steps that make a big difference.

The Power of Positive Thinking

Positive thinking might sound a bit like a cliché, but trust me, it's powerful stuff. It's not about ignoring the bad things or pretending everything's perfect – it's about changing your perspective. Try to find a silver lining in tough situations. Focus on the good stuff in your life, no matter how small.

Positive thinking is like a muscle – the more you use it, the stronger it gets. It can seriously transform your outlook on life, making challenges feel more like opportunities. And when you're positive, you attract positive vibes. It's kind of like being a posi- tivity magnet!

Celebrating Small Victories

In the journey of healing, every step forward is worth cele- brating. Got out of bed when you didn't feel like it? That's a win. Spoke up about your feelings? Another win. Each small victory is a step towards healing and rebuilding.

Celebrating these moments helps you recognize your progress. It's like giving yourself a pat on the back for being awesome. It rein- forces that you're moving forward, no matter the pace. So, cheer for yourself, do a little dance, treat yourself. You're doing amazing, and every small victory is proof of that!

Physical Wellness and Healing

You know how when you feel good physically, it kind of lifts your whole mood? That's the power of physical wellness. After a rough time in a toxic relationship, taking care of your body is super important. Regular exercise – like jogging, yoga, or even just dancing in your room – can seriously boost your mood. It's like, every time you move, you're shaking off some of that heavy stuff you've been carrying.

Eating right is another biggie. It's not about strict diets or anything – just about fueling your body with stuff that makes you feel ener- gized and good. Think fruits, veggies, nuts, and yeah, the occa- sional treat because balance is key! When your body feels nourished, it's like giving a high-five to your emotional well-being.

Establishing Routine and Structure

Okay, so routines might sound boring, but hear me out. After being in a chaotic relationship, having a bit of structure in your day can be like a soothing balm. It gives you a sense of control and normalcy. Like, maybe you start your day with a short walk, have specific times for study, and wind down with a book at night. It's all about creating a rhythm in your day that feels comforting and stable.

A routine can be a powerful tool to ground you, especially when things feel overwhelming. It's like setting up signposts throughout your day to help guide you along. And hey, it's totally okay to switch it up when you need to. Flexibility within structure – that's the magic combo!

Future Planning and Goal Setting

Ever heard of that saying, "A goal without a plan is just a wish"? It's so true. Planning for your future and setting goals can give you a sense of direction after a toxic relationship. Start with small, achievable goals. Maybe it's getting a certain grade, learning a new skill, or just practicing self-care daily.

Write your goals down and break them into steps. It's like creating a roadmap for where you want to go. Every small step you take is a move toward a future that you're in charge of. Remember, these are your goals, your dreams – you're the artist here, painting your future. And it's okay if your goals change over time; flexibility is part of growth.

AMPING UP YOUR CONFIDENCE GAME

1. Discover Your Strengths: You're Awesome, Own It!

First things first, let's focus on what makes you, well, you. You've got strengths and talents that are unique to you. Maybe you're a whiz at math, a creative artist, a patient listener, or the person who can always make others laugh. Discover these gems and polish them. Remember, confidence starts with recognizing what you're good at.

Detail in your mind a list of the good things about you. Then repeat them as affirmations.

For instance, "I am a great friend! My friendship is valuable."

2. Step Out of Your Comfort Zone: Where the Magic Happens

Okay, so stepping out of your comfort zone can be scary, but it's also where you grow. Try new things – join a club, learn a new skill, speak up in class. Each time you push those boundaries, you're building your confidence. It's like leveling up in a video game. Each new challenge you conquer makes you stronger and more confident.

3. Positive Self-Talk: Be Your Own Cheerleader

You know that little voice in your head? Make sure it's your biggest fan, not your biggest critic. Replace thoughts like "I can't do this" with "I'll give it my best shot." Positive self-talk is a game- changer. It's like having an invisible cheerleader who's always there to pump you up.

4. Body Language: Strike a Power Pose

Your body language says a lot about how you feel. Standing tall, making eye contact, and smiling can actually make you feel more confident. It's like tricking your brain into feeling power- ful. Before a big moment – a test, a presentation, a sports game – strike a power pose. Stand with your hands on your hips and your head held high. Feel the confidence surge through you!

5. Set Small Goals: Baby Steps to Big Wins

Set yourself small, achievable goals. It could be as simple as talking to someone new, completing a project, or learning part of a new skill. Each small win adds up and boosts your confidence. It's like collecting coins in a video game – the more you collect, the stronger you become.

6. Reflect on Your Progress: Look How Far You've Come!

Take time to reflect on what you've achieved. It's easy to forget your wins when you're always looking ahead. Reflecting on your progress shows you how capable you are and builds your confi- dence. Keep a journal or a list on your phone – somewhere you can see your victories and remind yourself, "Hey, I did that!"

7. Surround Yourself with Positive People: Your Squad Matters

The people you hang out with can influence how you feel about yourself. Stick with friends who lift you up, who believe in you, and who make you feel good about yourself. Ditch the negativity. Positive vibes from your squad can boost your confidence like nothing else.

Remember, building confidence doesn't happen overnight. It's a journey. There will be ups and downs, but every step you take is a step towards a more confident you. Believe in yourself – you've got this!

SELF-EMPOWERMENT: JUMP IN THE DRIVER'S SEAT

Grab the Wheel – Your Guide to Self-Empowerment

Ever felt like life's a car, and you're stuck in the passenger seat? Well, it's time to slide into the driver's seat and take control! Self- empowerment is all about steering your own life, making your own choices, and being your own hero. Let's get into what it means to be empowered and how you can totally rock it.

Self-Empowerment: What's the Deal?

Imagine you're behind the wheel of a car. That's your life. Self- empowerment means you're in charge of the direction you're going, the turns you take, and the speed you're driving at. It's about making decisions for yourself and standing up for what you believe in. If someone else, like a toxic partner, has been driving your car, it's time to kindly ask them to get out or hop into the backseat – this is your car and only you have the right to drive it!

The Power of Knowing Yourself

Empowerment starts with self-awareness. It's like knowing every button, switch, and gauge on your car's dashboard. Understanding your worth, your strengths, and your values is super important. Think about Lizzo – the queen of self-love anthems. She's all about embracing who you are and living your best life. Her songs are like fuel for your empowerment journey!

Practical Steps to Empowerment

Discover Your Passions: What lights you up? Painting? Music? Science? Dive into what you love, and let it empower you.

Set Personal Goals: Goals are like destinations on a GPS. Set some cool ones, and start driving towards them. They could be small, like finishing a book, or big, like running for student council.

Learn to Say No: Just like deciding not to take a wrong turn, saying 'no' is a powerful way to control your journey. Remember, 'no' is a complete sentence!

Speak Up: Your voice matters. Whether it's in class, with friends, or at home, share your thoughts and opinions.

You've got some awesome stuff to say!

Build a Support Crew: Surround yourself with people who cheer you on. Think of them as your road trip buddies, there for the laughs, the cries, and the sing-alongs. **Practice Self-Care:** Taking care of yourself is key. It's like keeping your car well-maintained. Do things that make you feel good, both inside and out.

Celebrate Your Wins: Every step forward, no matter how

small, is a victory. Treat yourself to a metaphorical victory lap around the track!

Your Journey, Your Rules

At the end of the day, your life is your story. Self-empowerment is about writing it in your own words, with your own pen. So, go ahead, grab that steering wheel with both hands, rev up your engine, and start driving towards your dreams. You're capable, you're strong, and you totally got this. Let's hit the road to empowerment!

ASSERTIVENESS – YOUR POWER TO SPEAK UP

What is Assertiveness?

Assertiveness is like finding the perfect volume on your music player. Not too loud (aggressive) and not too soft (passive), but just right. It's about saying what you need and how you feel, while also respecting others. It's about being honest and direct, but also kind and understanding.

Assertiveness is not about being bossy or pushy; it's about expressing your thoughts, needs, and feelings in a clear, honest, and respectful way. It's about standing up for yourself without stepping on anyone's toes.

Scenario: Group Projects – No More Being the Silent Sufferer

Imagine you're in a group project, and you're stuck with all the work while your mates chill. An assertive move? Call a group meeting and say, "Hey, I've noticed I'm taking on a lot of the project. Can we redistribute the tasks so it's fairer?" Boom. You've expressed your concern without blaming and opened the door for a fair solution.

Scenario: Setting Boundaries – Your Time, Your Rules

Let's say a friend always texts you late at night to vent. You want to help, but you also need your sleep. Being assertive here means setting a boundary. Try saying, "I'm here for you, but I can't respond to messages after 10 PM. Let's chat in the morning?" You're setting your limits while still being a caring friend.

Scenario: Peer Pressure – Steering Clear of the Uncool

You're at a party and someone's pressuring you to try something you're not comfortable with. Time to channel your inner assertiveness. Stand your ground with, "No thanks, I'm good without it." You're respecting your values and showing others you can't be easily swayed.

Scenario: Expressing Feelings – Crush Confession Time

Got a crush and want to express your feelings? Assertiveness to the rescue! Let's say you tell them, "I really enjoy spending time with you, and I've developed feelings for you. I'd love to hang out more." You're being open about your feelings without any pressure.

Practice Makes Perfect

Building assertiveness is like working out at a gym – the more you practice, the stronger you get. Start with small things, like voicing your restaurant preference or speaking up when you disagree in a discussion. Each little victory adds up, making you more confident in expressing yourself.

Remember, being assertive is a skill – and like any skill, it takes practice. But once you get the hang of it, it's incredibly empower- ing. It's about finding your voice and using it wisely. So, stand tall, speak up, and let your awesome assertiveness shine!

MENTAL RESILIENCE

Let's dive into something really cool: resilience. You know, that awesome power that lets you bounce back from tough times? We're talking about turning the tough stuff from toxic relation- ships into strengths that make you even more amazing.

What's resilience? It's not just about getting back up. It's about learning and growing from what knocked you down. Ever heard of Greta Thunberg? She's faced tons of challenges but keeps on fighting for what she believes. That's resilience in action.

How does it help with toxic relationships? It's like a shield. Helps you recover faster and guards you against future drama.

Flex that resilience muscle. Just like working out, the more you practice resilience, the stronger you get. And when you find your voice again, you're unstoppable!

Building Blocks of Resilience

- **Understand your feels.** Apps like Calm and Headspace? Perfect for figuring out your emotions.
- **Self-care is key.** Yoga, running, chilling with friends, or just jamming to your fave music. Self-care keeps your mind healthy.
- **Build your squad.** Having friends, family, or cool online peeps in places like r/teenrelationships can be a huge help.
- **Trust your feelings and emotions**.
- **Support yourself even when others don't.** Hey, why take other people's sides? Why not side with yourself and support your wants, needs, and feelings?

Beating Toxic Relationships

- **Acknowledge those feels.** It's totally okay to be hurt or upset. Recognizing it is your first step.

- **Learn from the past.** Think back to your old relationships. What went wrong? Learning this helps you dodge similar situations in the future.
- **Focus on what's next.** Don't get stuck in the past. You've got a bright future ahead, full of new adventures and people who get you.
- **Be brave.** Say no to things you don't want to do. Leave people who make you feel shitty. Make decisions, set boundaries, and stick to them. Set goals and stick to them. This can be scary at first, but all you really need is to make up your mind, be brave, and go through with it!

So, there you go! Embrace resilience like your fave superhero cape. It's about turning your experiences into power, learning from the past, and totally rocking your future. You've got this, and remem- ber, you're absolutely unstoppable!

19

AVOIDING HEARTBREAK ON REPEAT

TRUSTING YOUR INTUITION: THAT GUT FEELING

Imagine you're hanging out with someone new, but something just feels weird. You can't put your finger on it, but you just feel...uneasy, unhappy, maybe even a bit tense.

You're not sure what it is, but your gut is like, "Hey, pay attention!"

That's your intuition talking, and it's super important to listen to it. Your emotions are like your inner alarm system. They tell you when something's not quite right. Even if you can't explain why you feel a certain way, trust those feelings. They're there for a reason.

Your Body Knows: Ever been around someone and suddenly, you get a headache, or your stomach starts doing

242 | JORDAN PHOENIX

backflips? That's your body picking up on vibes and reacting. It's another way your intu- ition speaks to you. If you're feeling physically off around someone – like that weird knot in your stomach when they make a so-called 'joke' – it's a big hint that something's up.

Learning from the Past: Think back to a time when you were in a not-so-great relationship. Maybe your ex used to put you down 'as a joke.' Now, if you notice someone new acting a bit like your ex, that's your intuition waving a red flag. Reflecting on what you've been through before helps you spot those warning signs early. It's like having a mental checklist: "Have I seen this kind of thing before? Yep, I have, and it wasn't cool."

So, whenever you're feeling unsure, remember to trust that inner voice. It's like having a superpower that helps you navigate the world of relationships, friendships, and all that comes with them. Listen to it, because more often than not, your gut knows what's up!

RECOGNIZING RED FL AGS IN NEW REL ATIONSHIPS

1. **When They're Rude for No Reason**: Imagine you're on a date, and everything's going smoothly, but then your date is super rude to the waiter over something small. That's a major red flag for disrespectful

behavior. Respect is key, and someone who's genuinely into you will treat you and others with kindness, not like they're better than everyone else.

2. **Over-the-Top Jealousy**: Picture this: You're at a party, chatting with an old buddy, and your partner gets all moody and accuses you of flirting. Big red flag! A bit of jealousy can happen, but if it's intense and makes you feel like you're always doing something wrong, that's not okay. A cool partner trusts you and knows you can have friends without any drama.

3. **Playing Mind Games**: Say you're video chatting, and your part- ner's giving you this sob story, making you feel like you have to fix everything for them. Watch out – that's manipulative behavior. A partner who's constantly playing the victim or making you feel guilty isn't being straight with you. You want someone who's real with you, not someone who's trying to twist your feelings.

4. **They Just Don't Get You**: You've had a super bad day, and when you tell your partner, they're like, "Just get over it." That's a sign they might not have much empathy. Being with someone means getting where they're coming from, especially when times are tough. You deserve someone who's there for you, listens, and actu- ally gets how you feel.

5. **Any of that other toxic stuff we spoke about!**Remember, dating should be about feeling

244 | JORDAN PHOENIX

good and respected, not dealing with someone who makes everything a drama or mess. Keep an eye out for these red flags and trust your gut – you know what's best for you!

PASSING THE TORCH OF HOPE

You've journeyed through the pages, discovered secrets to escape toxic chains, and now you're standing in the light of newfound wisdom. It's your turn to be the beacon for others who are still navigating through the darkness.

By sharing your genuine thoughts about this book on Amazon, you're not just leaving a review; you're guiding lost souls to a safe harbor. Your words can be a signpost for fellow teens searching for a way out of the shadows of harmful relationships.

Your support means the world. It's how we spread the message of hope and healing far and wide. By passing on your insights, you're contributing to a safer, kinder world for teens everywhere.

Thank you for being an integral part of this mission. With each person you reach, you're helping to strengthen the chain of posi- tive change.

Together, we're not just reading about change; we're making it happen.

Jordan Phoenix

Click here to share your journey and light the way for others on Amazon.

https://www.amazon.com/review/create-review/?ie=UTF8&channel=glance-detail&asin=

20

BUILDING HEALTHY REL ATIONSHIPS

Alright, let's dive into how you can grow some beautiful, healthy relationships after experiencing the not-so-great ones. Think of this as your guide to nurturing relationships that make you feel awesome, respected, and totally understood.

Blueprint of a Healthy Relationship: Imagine a relationship where there's loads of respect, trust, honesty, and you can chat about anything. That's what you're aiming for. It's like building a super cool treehouse where both of you are bringing in the best planks and nails – trust, respect, and real talk.

Setting Boundaries: This is like drawing your own personal map where you mark out your no-go zones. Boundaries are your way of telling people how you wanna be treated.

They're not just good for you; they keep your relationships healthy and balanced. Remember, it's totally cool to say no sometimes. Boundaries aren't just fences; they're the gates to a happier you.

Emotional Intelligence is Your Superpower: Being able to figure out what you're feeling and why is like having a secret decoder ring for life. It helps you understand others better, avoid misun- derstandings, and keep your relationships smooth sailing. Apps like "Mood Meter" can be super helpful in getting your emotional intelligence game on point.

Empathy: The Magic Glue: Empathy is about getting how someone else feels, like really stepping into their shoes. It can turn a "meh" relationship into something amazing. It's like having a magic glue that binds you and others in a really cool, under- standing way.

Building healthy relationships is about mixing all these ingredients – respect, boundaries, emotional smarts, and empathy – to create something that's good for you and the people around you. It's your recipe for relationships that rock!

HAPPY FRIENDSHIPS

The Roots of Great Relationships

Picture this: You're in a cool, calm forest. There's this tree that's been there forever, super strong and reliable. That's what a solid friend is like – always there, a constant in your life. In a relation- ship, this kind of stability and trust is key. You want someone who's got your back, rain or shine.

A real-deal friend is someone who tells you the hard truths. They're honest, even when it stings a bit, because they care. In a romantic relationship, that honesty builds a trust that's rock-solid.

Now, think empathy. A friend who gets you, feels with you, and understands your highs and lows – that's gold. When this trans- lates into a romantic relationship, it's like a super- power. You're not just lovers; you're emotionally in sync, feeling each other's vibes.

Respect is massive. Good friends respect who you are, your space, and your choices. They don't try to mold you into someone else. In a romantic relationship, this respect is everything. It means loving each other for who you truly are, not some fantasy version.

And don't forget the fun factor. Friends who light up your world, who crack you up and lift you up – they're keepers. In a romance, this means being with someone who makes your heart happy, who brings sunshine to your cloudiest days.

Talking It Out: The Heart-to-Heart Connection

Imagine a bridge. It's not just any bridge – it's one that lets you cross over to really understand someone. That's what talking and listening in a friendship (and more-than-friendship) are like. You're building a connection that lets all the important stuff flow back and forth.

Being clear and open in your chats, saying what you think and feel, and doing it with respect – that's crucial. And listening – really listening – to what they're saying is just as important. It's about getting each other, not just nodding along.

Your body talks too, you know. A glance, a smile, the way you tilt your head – it's all part of the conversation. Being clued into these can make you a communication ninja.

So, remember, a fab friendship (and an awesome romance) is built on this kind of talking and listening. It's about being there for each other, being real, and having those heart-to-hearts that make everything better.

Fixing Friendship Fumbles: Like Kintsugi for Relationships

Ever heard of Kintsugi? It's this awesome Japanese art where broken pottery is fixed with gold. The idea is that the breaks are part of its story, making it even cooler. That's kinda like sorting out conflicts in friendships. When things get rocky, it's a chance to make your bond even stronger.

So, when a clash pops up, think of it as a growth spurt for your friendship. Speak your mind, but keep it cool with "I feel" stuff. Like, "I feel upset when..." instead of pointing fingers. It's all about getting your feelings out there without making it a blame game.

Really hearing what your mate is saying is key. Get where they're coming from and let them know you get it. It's not about winning an argument; it's about fixing things up so everyone's cool.

And hey, saying sorry and letting go of hard feelings? That's huge. Grudges just drag you down, but forgiveness? That's like a friend- ship superpower.

Keeping Friendships Fresh and Fab

Picture a garden with all these amazing flowers. They didn't just pop up overnight; they needed some serious TLC. That's what friendships are like. You've got to put in the effort to keep them awesome.

Hang out with your pals (and boo) regularly. It could be grabbing a coffee, hitting a movie, or just shooting a text. It's all about making those memories and keeping the good vibes flowing.

Show some love to your friends. A simple "thanks" or a little surprise can make their day. It's all about making them feel special and showing you care.

Be there when things get tough. Sometimes, just being there to listen or give a hug is all it takes. Your support can be a total game- changer when your friend's going through a rough patch.

Remember, friendships are like those flowers in the garden. They need your time, your care, and a whole lot of love to really bloom. So, keep on watering them with kindness and watch as they grow into something beautiful and strong.

HAPPY ROMANCE

Getting the Love Languages Down

Ever tried playing a video game in a language you don't know? Super confusing, right? But once you figure out the controls, it's like unlocking a secret level. That's what understanding love languages in a relationship is like.

Gary Chapman, this total love guru, talks about these five love languages: Words of Affirmation, Quality Time, Receiving Gifts, Acts of Service, and Physical Touch. Everyone has a fave one. It's like, how do you get those lovey-dovey feels? Knowing your part- ner's love language is like knowing their cheat code to happiness. And don't forget to show them yours too. It's like swapping your playlists – you get to know what jams make each other groove.

Real Talk: The Heartbeat of Your Relationship

Communication in a relationship? Think of it as the Wi-Fi connection. Strong signal, everything's smooth. Weak signal, and it's buffering city. It's all about being real with each other. Share your stories, your dreams, your kinda-wanna-hide-this stuff. It makes your bond like, super strong. And hey, listening's part of the deal too. So tune in like you're listening to your favorite podcast.

Respect + Understanding = Strong Relationship Game

Picture a super cool bridge, like the Golden Gate. Now, think of mutual respect and understanding as the mega towers holding it up. Respect is about treating each other like rock stars. You get their quirks, you don't cross lines, and you're all about lifting each other up.

Understanding? That's like putting on their sneakers and walking a mile. It's about getting where they're coming from. When you mix respect with understanding, you've got this solid foundation. Even when things get shaky, like big-time disagreements, your relationship bridge stays strong.

Grooving Together, Rocking Solo: The Relationship Dance

Ever watched a dance where everyone's in sync, but still rocking their own moves? That's what balancing your space and together- ness in a relationship is all about. It's like being in a squad where everyone's vibe is different, but you all still jam together.

On one side, there's the 'us' time – like, binge-watching your fave series, going on wild adventures, or just chilling and making memories. Then, there's the 'me' time – you know, jamming on your guitar, hanging with your crew, or just doing your own thing.

The trick is to get this happy mix where you're totally into each other but still doing your own thing. Think of it like a playlist where you've got some duets and some solo tracks. This way, your relationship is like this epic dance party where you both feel plugged in together but still get to freestyle.

Mixtape of Love: The Ultimate Relationship Playlist

Getting a romantic relationship right is like being a DJ for the coolest party. You've got to know what tunes your partner digs (their love language), keep the convo flowing like the sickest beats (communication), and respect each other like headliner artists (mutual respect).

And when it comes to hanging together vs. doing your own thing, it's all about finding that perfect rhythm.

That's how you roll in a healthy romantic relationship – under- standing each other's love languages, keeping the communication real, and building your love on the solid ground of respect and understanding.

Conclusion: Your Story, Your Power

Hey there, amazing person! If you're reading this, hats off to you. You're not just flipping through pages; you're taking huge strides on a brave journey. Seriously, I'm super proud of you for diving into understanding and healing from tough stuff like toxic rela- tionships. That takes guts!

The Big Lessons You've Learned: We've been through a lot together in this book, right? Spotting toxic vibes, dealing with the rollercoaster of emotions, picking up the pieces, and learning how not to fall into the same traps again. Every bit of this journey

shows just how strong and resilient you are. Remember, healing's more like a road trip than a quick sprint. It's all about the journey, not just the destination.

What's Next on Your Adventure: So, what now? Well, it's your epic story, and you're the hero holding the pen. Time to write your next chapter, your fresh start. Take all those lessons and turn them into your superpowers. Set those boundaries, give yourself some major love, and build that toughness. And hey, be cool with your- self. Celebrate every tiny win and believe that you can make things better.

Embracing Change: Your Superpower: Change can be super freaky, I get it. But guess what? It's also where the magic happens. You're like a butterfly getting ready to show off its colors. That power to change and grow? It's all you, buddy.

You're not just your past or the tough times you've faced. Nope, you're defined by your bravery to heal, your strength to keep going, and your huge heart, still full of kindness and love.

Your Story, Their Hope: Your story? It's a powerful thing – like a guiding light for others who might feel lost. When you feel ready, think about sharing it. You never know who you might inspire or comfort. Whether it's chatting with a friend, a post on Insta, or joining a group, every story shared helps in ways you can't even imagine.

You've journeyed so far, and trust me, this is just the start. What's ahead? A whole lot of discovering who you are, healing, and turning into the best version of yourself. It's not always going to be smooth sailing, but it's going to be so worth it. Because you, my friend, are absolutely worth every effort.

So here's a toast to you – brave, unstoppable, beautiful you. To your journey, your healing, and all the amazing chapters of your life that are still waiting to be written. You've totally got this.

Remember, you're not alone in this. You're a warrior on an epic journey, and every step you take is a victory. Keep shining, keep growing, and keep being the awesome person you are!

YOU ARE WORTHY OF LOVE!

I just want you to know something really important – you are absolutely amazing, just the way you are. I know things might seem super tough right now, but trust me, you have this incredible strength inside you, and you are so worthy of all the good things life has to offer.

You know what? You are capable of so much more than you real- ize. Every dream, every goal, every little wish you have – you can make it happen. Because you, my friend, are unstoppable when you set your mind to something.

Remember this: you are lovable, just as you are. You don't have to change a thing to earn that love. You're already good inside, a beautiful soul shining bright. You have this inner value and worth that nobody can take away from you, no matter what.

Guess what? You deserve good things – to be treated with kind- ness and respect, to have joy and happiness in your life. And your thoughts, feelings, opinions? They matter so much. They're just as important as anyone else's. Never let anyone tell you otherwise.

Even if you feel like you're stuck in a dark place right now, I promise you it can and will get brighter. You have the power to pull yourself into the light, to carve out a future filled with happiness and love. What happened to you is just one part of your story – it's not the end, and it definitely doesn't define you.

You deserve a future that's as bright and wonderful as you are. A future where you're treated with the love and respect you so rightly deserve. What happened in the past? It's a chapter in your book, but you're the one who gets to write the rest of the story. And I know it's going to be an incredible one.

So, here's to your journey ahead. It's going to have ups and downs, but through it all, you're going to grow, learn, and come out stronger. Remember, every step you take is a step towards a future where you're cherished, valued, and loved.

Keep believing in yourself, because I believe in you with all my heart. You've got this, and I'm right here cheering you on every step of the way. Here's to you – the brave, the resilient, the beau- tiful you. Your future is bright, and it's waiting for you to seize it. Go out there and shine like the star you are!

CONCLUSION

You've made it to the end of our journey together in this book. That's seriously awesome, and I'm super proud of you. Let's do a quick recap of the epic stuff we've covered, okay?

What We Explored:

Toxic Relationships: We dug deep into what they look like, feel like, and how they mess with your head and heart. **Breaking Free:** Remember how we talked about spotting those bad vibes and saying 'no more'?

Building You Back Up: We've been all about boosting your confidence and self-esteem after being in a rough spot.

Moving On: Learning to let go and stride into a future that's way brighter.

Healthy Relationships: We chatted about what a cool, healthy relationship should look like and how you can totally have one.

Different Types of Relationships: Not just the romantic ones, but also friendships and family ties.

Empower Yourself: You've learned how to set boundaries, speak up for yourself, and take control of your life.

Resilience: That superhero ability to bounce back stronger.

Avoiding the Bad Stuff: You're now equipped to dodge toxic relationships and build healthier ones.

Big Takeaways for You:

- **Toxic relationships? They're everywhere.** Not just in dating, but with friends and family too.
- **Healing is a journey.** It takes time, effort, and a whole lot of self-love.
- **You're the boss of your life.** Setting boundaries and respecting yourself? That's your superpower.
- **Stay positive and resilient.** It's your secret weapon in healing and growing.

Your Next Steps:

Read the bonus guide on how to heal from the damaging effect of a toxic relationship. It's like a toolkit full of really powerful stuff to help you get rid of harmful negative beliefs, rebuild trust in yourself, feel better about yourself, and break the chains tying you to your abusive partner.

Keep applying what we've talked about. Real life is the ultimate test, and I know you're gonna ace it.

Remember, this book might be ending, but your journey? It's just getting started. You've got a whole world of experiences waiting for you.

And One Last Thing:

If you've found something in here that's helped you, sparked a thought, or given you a 'lightbulb' moment, why not share it? Maybe on your Insta, Twitter, or just with a friend. You never know who else it might help.

So, here's to you – for being brave, for being open, and for being on this journey. You're not just surviving; you're thriving. And I can't wait to see all the amazing places you'll go from here. Keep shining bright, and always remember: You've got this!"

BEGIN THE HEALING PROCESS FROM A TOXIC TEENAGE RELATIONSHIP

A GUIDE AND WORKBOOK OF POSITIVE AFFIRMATIONS, SELF-REFLECTION, AND JOURNAL WRITING

JORDAN PHOENIX, MA

HEALING FROM A TOXIC RELATIONSHIP

Hey there! You've already taken an amazing journey through our main book, diving deep into understanding toxic relationships and how to heal from them. But we're not done yet – this guide is your next step to really making those changes.

Think of this guide as your personal toolbox, filled with exercises, prompts, and affirmations, all designed to help you apply everything you've learned. Each activity is a step forward in your healing process, from strengthening your self-esteem to building healthier relationships.

You're all set to take on something big – those unseen ties that pull us into not-so-great relationships. Yep, I've been right where you are.

Think of this not just as a book but as your new journey. A step out of the tangles of toxicity into a world where you're in charge. This isn't about blame or being stuck in yesterday. It's about getting the lowdown, healing up, and stepping forward. We can't rewind what's done, but what comes next? That's all you.

I'm here as your guide, not as some know-it-all, but as someone who's walked the walk. I've felt the whole mess of it – the hurt, the mixed-up feelings, and yeah, the awesome feeling of breaking free.

If you ever come across a term or concept that seems a bit fuzzy, don't hesitate to flip back to the main book, "A Teenager's Guide to Recovery from Toxic Relationships – Regain Your Confidence in Weeks – A Step-By-Step Journey to Healthy Relationships and Narcissistic Behavior Awareness" for a quick refresher. Remember, healing is a journey, and this guide is here to support you every step of the way.

You're not alone in this, okay? Your feelings are totally legit. And there's a way through this maze. But hey, it's totally normal to feel a bit rattled or like you don't have all the answers. Recovery is more of a road trip than a quick hop. And every road trip kicks off with that first mile.

Ready to hit the road? 'Cause I totally believe in you. You've got what it takes to shake off those invisible ties and have a happier future. Let's dive in.

1

GASLIGHTING

When you're being gaslit, it can feel like you're in a dark maze without any way out. You doubt your memory, thoughts, feelings, and sanity.

UN-GASLIGHTING YOURSELF

Well, guess what happens when you break free from being gaslit? It's like the maze just starts shrinking! Yep, it shrinks and shrinks until you can finally stand up tall, look around, and see the real world for what it truly is.

Becoming un-gaslit is like unlocking this epic level of freedom and self-discovery. It's about realizing the amazing person you are, away from all those fake, dark illusions your abuser threw over you like some sort of wicked spell. The moment you toss aside those bewitched black sunglasses, everything changes. You can see clearly, and suddenly, you're not under their spell anymore.

It's like you've been playing this game with a blindfold, and now it's off. You're seeing colors, lights, and paths you never knew existed. You're free from their control, free to choose your own way, and free to be the incredible person you always were underneath their tricks.

So let's take off and keep off those sunglasses. The world's a lot brighter and a lot more beautiful when you see it with your own eyes, free from anyone else's control. You've got this, and the adventure ahead is all yours!

MEMORY VALIDATION EXERCISE

Developing self-confidence in your own memories and thoughts can be strengthened through reflective thinking and journaling.

Here are some questions and exercises that can help you build trust in your own mind. This will help you be un-gaslit and realize your memories are valid and deserve to be considered.

Mentally consider the answer these questions:

1. **Past Memory Wins:** Think about times when you remembered something spot-on, and it turned out you were totally right. What does this say about how reliable your memory can be?

2. **Your Memory Superpowers:** What stuff do you remember best? Numbers, convo details, events, faces? Realizing where you're a memory whiz can totally boost your confidence.

3. **Check Your Records:** Got old diaries, emails, or photos? See how they match up with what you remember. What does it say about your memory accuracy?

4. **Smart Decisions, Smart Thoughts:** Reflect on choices you made based on your thoughts that led to cool stuff happening. This proves your brain's on the right track!

5. **Learning from Oops Moments:** Ever realized you goofed in your thinking and then fixed it? This shows you're good at evaluating and trusting your brain.

6. **Intuition Wins:** Recall times when a gut feeling or sudden idea steered you right. These moments prove your inner guidance system is legit.

7. **Props from Your Peeps**: Remember when friends or family said, "Wow, you remembered!" or you rocked a memory game or quiz? This external high-five backs up your memory skills.

8. **Perfectly Imperfect Memory**: Everyone's memory messes up sometimes. It's totally normal, and it doesn't mean your memory is unreliable overall.

9. **How You Handle Info**: Think about how you process stuff. Do you take your time? Look at different sides of a story? This careful approach helps make your memories more accurate.

10. **Doubt vs. Evidence Showdown**: When you doubt a memory, do you look for proof or think it through logically to back it up?

11. **Chill Time with Good Memories**: Spend some time just thinking about when your memory was your superhero. How did it feel? How did it help?

12. **Consistent Thoughts**: Consider how consistent your thoughts are over time. Are your beliefs and opinions generally stable and make sense?

Building Trust with Your Brain

By diving into these exercises, you're giving your brain a high-five. You're recognizing all the cool stuff it does right, which can help shake off doubts and boost your confidence in your own thoughts and memories. Remember, your brain is like your internal Google, and it's usually pretty spot on. So trust it, and watch your self- confidence grow!

Keep exploring your mind's capabilities, and remember, your thoughts and memories are a big part of what makes you, you! Trust in them, and trust in yourself. You've got this!

TRUSTING YOUR MEMORY

Building trust in your own memories, mind, and feelings is essential for your self-confidence and mental well-being. Here are some empowering affirmations tailored for this purpose:

1. **"My memories are a valid part of my experience."**
2. **"I trust my memory and my ability to recall events accurately."**
3. **"My mind is clear, strong, and reliable."**
4. **"I believe in the integrity of my thoughts and feelings."**
5. **"Every day, my confidence in my mental abilities grows stronger."**
6. **"I am capable of discerning the truth in my experiences."**
7. **"My perceptions are grounded in reality and truth."**
8. **"I respect and honor my experiences and memories."**
9. **"I am mentally strong and independent."**
10. **"My thoughts and memories are an important part of who I am."**

11. "I have the inner wisdom to interpret my past accurately."
12. "I am in control of my mental processes and trust in their accuracy."
13. "My mind is a powerful ally in understanding my life's journey."
14. "I embrace my experiences with clarity and confidence."
15. "Each day, my trust in my own mind becomes firmer."
16. "I am at peace with my memories and trust my interpretation of them."
17. "My feelings and memories are acknowledged and respected by me."

Using these affirmations regularly can help reinforce your belief in yourself and your mental capabilities. Whenever you feel doubtful, repeat these affirmations to remind yourself of your ability to trust your own mind and memories. It's also helpful to keep a journal of your thoughts and experiences as a way to validate and strengthen your trust in your own perceptions and memories.

YOU, ME, YES, NO, MAYBE, OH!

Who is the crazy one? They blame you, they say you can't remember stuff or are making stuff up. But who is really at fault here? Let's find out.

Answer these 6 questions to unravel the truth:

1. **Single Source Doubt**: Is it only [partner's name] who says you have a bad memory or are making things up? Think about it, do your friends or family say the same?

2. **Friends' Perspectives**: What do your friends think about your memory and perceptions? Do they ever doubt your sanity like [partner's name] does?

3. **Pre-Relationship Confidence**: Try to remember, before you met [partner's name], did you ever doubt your memory this much? If not, why do you think that's changed?

4. **Imagine a Different Scenario**: If [partner's name] never told you that you can't remember stuff or are crazy, how would you view your own memory? Would you feel differently about your sanity?

5. **Flipping the Script**: Ever considered that maybe [partner's name] is the one who's got memory issues? How would it make you feel to find out they're the forgetful one, not you?

6. **Trustworthiness Question**: Why do you think [partner's name] is more reliable with memories than you? What makes their version automatically more credible?

(Do not answer with "because they say so!") Could it be that they're wrong?

Flipping the Perspective: Seeing the Bigger Picture

It's super important to realize that sometimes, the issue isn't with you but with the person making you doubt yourself. These questions are designed to help you see the pattern in your partner's behavior and understand that their actions might be a form of manipulation, not a reflection of your abilities.

Remember, understanding gaslighting is like solving a puzzle. It's about looking at all the pieces – your feelings, your memories, your partner's words – and seeing the real picture. Trust in your-self, your memories, and your sanity. You're smarter and stronger than you think, and you deserve to believe in yourself.

VALIDATING YOUR REALITY: STAND STRONG AGAINST GASLIGHTING

Exercises to Affirm Your Perception of Reality:

1. **Recall Clear Memories**: Think of a few moments where you're 100% sure of what happened. Reflect on these memories and remind yourself how clear and certain they felt.
2. **Reaffirm What You Know**: Write down things you know to be true about yourself and your life. These could be your talents, your values, or positive moments you've experienced.

3. **Compare Perspectives**: If someone's challenging your view of an event, jot down both versions. Seeing them side by side can help you stand firm in what you know is true.

4. **Seek Objective Input**: Talk to a trusted friend or family member about an event you're unsure of. Their outside perspective can help validate your reality.

5. **Document Your Experiences**: Keep a journal of events, feelings, and reactions. Reviewing this can help reinforce your memory and perception, especially when someone tries to challenge them.

6. **Identify Gaslighting Red Flags**: Make a list of common gaslighting phrases like "You're too sensitive" or "That never happened." Recognizing these can help you stay alert to manipulation attempts.

7. **Reflect on Consistency**: Consider how consistent your memories and perceptions have been over time. This can help reinforce your trust in them.

Affirmations to Strengthen Belief in Your Reality

1. **"I trust my memory and perception of events."**
2. **"My feelings and experiences are valid and real."**
3. **"I am confident in my understanding of my life and my experiences."**

276 | JORDAN PHOENIX

4. "I stand firm in my truth, even when others challenge it."
5. "I recognize and resist attempts to manipulate my perception of reality."
6. "My experiences and memories define my reality, not someone else's words."
7. "I am strong against gaslighting and trust in my inner voice."
8. "I seek truth and clarity in all situations."
9. "My perspective is valuable and deserves to be heard and respected."
10. "I am capable of discerning truth from manipulation." Embracing and Trusting Your Reality

By engaging with these exercises and repeating these affirmations, you're building a fortress of trust in your own perceptions and memories. Remember, your reality is shaped by your experiences, and you have the power to validate and trust it, no matter what others say.

Stay confident in your truth, and remember, your perspective is unique and invaluable. Trust in yourself, and you'll navigate through life's challenges with strength and clarity. You've got this!

2

EMOTIONAL ABUSE

Being insulted, called names, mocked, belittled, degraded, told you're not worthy, etc... that can really ruin your self-esteem and make you feel like you're not worthy of anything good. Know that those are just negative echoes from the abuse you suffered, NOT the truth. In this chapter, we'll help you get rid of those fake beliefs and increase your self-worth.

WORTHY, NOT WORTHY... WHICH IS TRUE?

When Insults Start to Sound Like 'Truth'

Ever notice how, when someone keeps dissing you, you start to wonder if they're onto something? You might think, "If they keep saying I'm [insert mean comment here], maybe it's true?"

278 | JORDAN PHOENIX

But here's the deal: just because someone says something doesn't make it your reality.

Their Words vs. Your Reality

Picture this: You're in an art gallery, right? There's this wild painting on the wall, all abstract and stuff. Three peeps are standing there, checking it out.

Person 1: "OMG, this is the most beautiful thing ever!"

Person 2: "Yuck, this is the ugliest painting I've ever seen!"

Person 3: "Meh, it's alright, kinda in the middle for me."

So, who's right? What's the 'truth' here?

Spoiler: There's no one 'truth' – it's all about perspective!

That painting isn't changing – it's the same bunch of colors and strokes. But to one person, it's a masterpiece; to another, it's a disaster; and to someone else, it's just meh. Their opinions don't change what the painting actually is; they're just different views.

Your Worth Isn't Defined by Their Opinion

Here's how this painting thing ties into real life. Let's talk about Judy. She's super skinny, and her first BF was all about trying to 'fatten her up.' He'd be like, "You're too skinny, you're all bones. I hate skinny girls!" Judy felt terrible, thinking she was ugly and unlovable.

But plot twist: They break up, and she meets Drew, who's totally into skinny girls. He's all, "You're gorgeous! I love your thin wrists, your ankles, everything!" For Drew, skinny is his type.

See, Judy didn't change – she's still the same person. But the opinions about her did. What her ex thought of her body was his deal, not hers. His words didn't define her beauty or worth; they were just his opinion, based on his likes and dislikes.

Questions to Get You Thinking

Q1: The Skinny on Worthiness

So, Judy's skinny – does that make her any less worthy of love? Think about it. Does her waist size have a VIP pass to her heart?

Q2: Change for Love – Yay or Nay?

Do you really think Judy needs to change herself to be loved? Is it about swapping her jeans size or finding someone who digs her style as is?

Q3: Makeover Time – Herself or Her Circle?

What's the real change needed for Judy – a new look or a new crew? Should she be flipping through fashion mags or flipping the script on who she hangs with?

Real Talk on Change

Who's Got the Issue? Spoiler: Not Judy

The problem isn't with Judy or her body; it's about being with someone who's not vibing with her as she is. You can't remix other people's tastes, but you can totally choose who you share your playlist with.

If someone's throwing shade your way, if they're not loving the awesome you, maybe it's not about a personal rebrand. Maybe it's about finding peeps who celebrate your brand of awesome. Trust me, they're out there!

The Affirmation You Gotta Repeat

"What they say about me is just their opinion. It's not the truth about who I am. Their words and what they think are totally not the same as my worth. I'm like this gem with my own sparkle, and that doesn't change with someone else's weather report.

I'm 100% lovable just as I am. No edits needed."

Remember, you're not a rough draft needing edits; you're a final print, perfect in your own story. Stay true to your plot – it's worth the read!

"WHY IS MY PARTNER ACTING LIKE A MONSTER?"

Ever wonder, "Why would my BF/GF want to hurt me?" Okay, so here's the thing: psychology is like this huge, complicated puzzle. Some peeps, including those who turn out to be not-so-great partners, have been through tough stuff themselves. They're carrying around this hurt, like thorns poking them from the inside. Ouch, right?

Sometimes, they don't know how to deal with these 'thorns,' so they lash out. Imagine that each time they get toxic or abusive, they're turning into this 'ugly monster.' This monster? It's not about them being evil; it's like a messed-up symbol of the pain and problems they haven't dealt with.

But here's the real talk: Their issues and their monster-like moments? They're not about you. They don't show your value; they show their struggles.

No Excuses for Being Cruel

And hey, important side note: Even if they've had a rough past, it's never, ever an excuse to treat you badly. You deserve respect and kindness, period. No buts or becauses – just straight-up love and respect.

MIRROR, MIRROR, NOT SO CLEAR: WHY THEY SAY HURTFUL STUFF

Okay, think about a mirror. Normally, it shows exactly what's in front of it. But if that mirror's all twisted or cracked, things get wonky. Like, imagine a tall, thin girl looking in this funky mirror and seeing herself all wavy and weird. That's not her; that's the mirror messing up the reflection.

That's kind of like what's going on with someone who's abusive. Their view of the world, and you, is like looking through a busted mirror. Their words and actions? They're coming from this distorted place filled with their own probs and insecurities.

So, when they say something hurtful, remember, it's like that wonky mirror. It's not showing you as you are; it's showing their messed-up version of reality.

You're Not Their Words

What they say, how they see you – that's on them, not you. Your worth, your smarts, your beauty – they're shining bright, no matter what they're spitting out. You're not the reflection in their cracked mirror; you're the real deal, all by yourself.

AFFIRMATIONS TO KEEP YOU GROUNDED

Affirmations are like spells; they're magic little sentences that help you feel better and increase your self-confidence. Simply repeat them multiple times out loud whenever you feel confused, hurt, unloved, and unsure about yourself.

- "I'm in charge of my actions, not theirs."
- "I'm not the reason for someone else's mean streak." "When they're mean, it's because they have a problem. It's not because of me."
- "It's not my fault someone is mean to me. It's their choices, their mess. Not mine."

Remember, you're your own person, not someone's shadow or a character in their messed-up story. Keep shining your light, and don't let anyone's inner monster dim it. You got this!

POSITIVITY EXERCISE: YOU VS. THEIR WORDS

Okay, so let's do a little exercise to help put some space between you and those hurtful words.

Step 1: Their Words on Paper

Grab a piece of paper and write down some of the stuff that's been said to you. Seeing it outside of your head can make a big difference.

Step 2: Who You Really Are

Now, on another piece of paper, write down all the amazing things about you. Your talents, your dreams, the compliments you've received, moments when you felt proud of yourself. Think of nice little things and big things that make you special.

This is the real you.

Step 3: Compare and Contrast

Hold those two pieces of paper side by side. See how different they are? That's because what people say about you doesn't define you. You're defined by your own strengths, achievements, and the love you carry in your heart.

Step 4: Trash Talk

Now, if you're feeling it, crumple up the first piece of paper – the one with the insults – and toss it in the trash. That's where it belongs. Not in your mind, not in your heart.

REFRAME IT!

Here's how to flip the script. Every time you catch yourself feeling down from an insult, pause. Ask yourself, 'What's something nice about me?' Remember, you're awesome, smart, funny... whatever makes you, you.

Start to see yourself through that lens of positivity, not through the negativity others throw at you.

AFFIRMATION REPLACEMENT EXERCISE

Step 1: Uncover Your Negative Beliefs

First, let's find out what negative beliefs might be lurking in your mind. Fill in the blanks in these questions to reveal them. Think about what you often feel or have been made to believe in your relationship:

1. "I'm not _____enough." (smart, good, pretty, etc.)
2. "I'm _____worthy of love." (un, not)
3. "I always _____" (mess up, fail, etc.)
4. "I don't deserve _____" (happiness, success, love)
5. "I'm too _____ to be loved." (flawed, different, etc.)

Write down these negative beliefs. Seeing them on paper can be powerful and eye-opening.

Step 2: Create Your Positive Affirmations

Now, for each negative belief you've written, let's flip it to create a positive affirmation. This is where you take back your power. Here's how you can transform them:

1. If you wrote, "I'm not smart enough," change it to: "**I am intelligent in my own unique way.**"
2. For "I'm unworthy of love," it becomes: "**I am worthy of love and respect.**"
3. If it's "I always mess up," turn it into: "**I learn and grow from every experience.**"
4. Change "I don't deserve happiness" to: "**I deserve happiness and joy in my life.**"
5. If you wrote, "I'm too flawed to be loved," it becomes: "**My flaws are part of my unique beauty, and I am lovable as I am.**"

Write these affirmations down as your new truths.

Step 3: Repeat Your Positive Affirmations

Now, repeat these positive affirmations to yourself. Do it every day, multiple times a day. Say them out loud, write them in your journal, put them on sticky notes around your room – whatever works for you.

- "I am intelligent in my own unique way."
- "I am worthy of love and respect."
- "I learn and grow from every experience."
- "I deserve happiness and joy in my life."
- "My flaws are part of my unique beauty, and I am lovable as I am."

Remember: You Are in Control

By repeating these affirmations, you're rewiring your brain to believe in your worth and value. You're taking control of your story, your self-view. It's a powerful way to heal and grow stronger.

You're not the negative things you've been made to believe. You're so much more. Keep using these affirmations to remind yourself of your true worth. You're amazing, just as you are!

Positive Affirmations Are like Your Secret Superpower

Your brain is like this super-smart computer.

And what you feed it makes a huge difference in how you feel and see the world.

When you repeat positive affirmations, it's like you're programming your brain to focus on the good stuff. It helps shift your mindset from "I can't" to "I totally got this." It's not magic, but it sure feels like it sometimes.

Write 'Em, Say 'Em, Believe 'Em

Grab a pen and some paper and write down some positive affirmations. They can be from the list we made or ones you come up with yourself. The key? They should be about how awesome, capable, and loved you are.

Then, make it a habit. Every morning, or whenever you need a pick-me-up, say these affirmations out loud. Look in the mirror and tell yourself these truths. It might feel weird at first, but give it time. You're planting seeds of positivity that will totally bloom.

Watch the Magic Happen

Over time, you'll start to notice a change. Those downer thoughts get a little quieter, and the positive ones start taking center stage. You'll feel more confident, more you. And that's when you realize: You've got the power to shape your world, one affirmation at a time.

POSITIVE AFFIRMATIONS

Whenever you feel down, repeat these positive affirmations out loud and write them down. You'll be amazed at how good it feels!

1. "I am worthy of respect and kindness."
2. "What someone says does not define me."
3. "My worth is not defined by their words."
4. "I am more than enough just as I am."
5. "I deserve a relationship that makes me feel good about myself."
6. "I am strong enough to stand up against negativity."
7. "My feelings and experiences are valid."
8. "I am capable of creating positive change in my life."
9. "I can achieve anything I want."
10. "I have inner value."

11. "I am good enough."
12. "I am valuable."

Affirmations are powerful and can totally transform your outlook. Keep those positive vibes flowing, and remember, you're the boss of your own thoughts. Rock on!

3

DEBUNKING NEGATIVE BELIEFS

YOU MATTER, AND I MATTER: THE TALE OF TWO APPLES

The Story of Big Red and Little Green

Imagine a tree, like the one you might chill under at the park. It's got loads of apples, each getting life-giving tree sap. They're all thriving, doing their apple thing.

But here's the drama: There's this one apple, let's call him Big Red. He's kinda the big shot of the branch. He's full of himself and feels really important.

One day, he's like, "Yo, I want ALL the sap, because I'm the MVP here. I matter more than all of you."

Next to him is this smaller, kinda shy apple, Little Green. He tries to speak up, but Big Red just shuts him down. "You? You don't matter, dude! It's all about what I want! Hand over your sap!"

Little Green gets all intimidated, feeling small and like he doesn't count. So, he lets Big Red take all his sap. Big Red gets bigger and shinier, while Little Green? He's just withering away, getting all shriveled and sad. Falling apart, starving to death...

What's Fair, What's Not

So, let's think about this. Is this fair? Does Big Red really deserve all the sap? What about Little Green? Doesn't he have a right to that life-giving sap too?

Little Green's over here thinking, "I guess I don't deserve the sap. Big Red said so. He's the important one, right? I just gave him what he wanted 'cause my needs don't matter."

Your Turn to Speak Up

Now, it's your turn to drop some truth bombs. What would you say to Little Green? How would you convince him that he matters just as much as Big Red?

Tell Little Green what you think:

Wrapping Up: Every Apple Deserves Sap

In the story of Big Red and Little Green, it's clear that every apple on that tree deserves its share of sap. Just like in life, everyone – including you – deserves respect, care, and the chance to thrive.

No one person's wants are more important than another person's wants. You matter just as much as your partner or anyone else.

You are just as worthy of love, respect, happiness, and all the good things you want as anyone else!

EMPOWERING AFFIRMATIONS

To strengthen yourself and be able to resist manipulation, it's important to realize that your opinions are just as valid as anyone else's. What you want matters just as much as what someone else wants.

Why should one person's wants be more important than another person's?

Why should their wants override someone else's?

To increase your self-confidence and not let others manipulate you anymore, repeat these affirmations often:

What one person says about me does not define what I am. I have inner value and worth no matter what someone says.

What they say doesn't define what I am. I am a great person always.

I am fully worthy of being treated with love and respect. My opinions are real, they matter, they are valid.

It's okay for me to have my own opinions. My opinions matter.

It's okay for me to do what I want. My wants and needs matter.

I matter.

I am important. I am valuable.

My feelings are just as important as [partner's name]. My opinions are just as valid as [partner's name].

I am just as important as [partner's name]. I matter just as much as anyone else.

Being unique is great. I don't need to be a copy of anyone else.

I am worthy of love even if I'm unique and different from anyone else.

"AM I WORTHY OF LOVE OR NOT?"

Jane's Wild Walk with the "Worthiness Meter"

Picture this: Jane's strutting down the street, and she's got this funky digital "worthiness meter" hovering over her head. And get this – she set it so ANYONE and everyone can mess with it. Why? 'Cause she thinks maybe they know her worth better than she does.

As she's walking, people are shouting their judgments at her, based on what? Their own likes and dislikes. One person's "NOT WORTHY," just 'cause they're not feeling her skirt. Another's like, "TOTALLY WORTHY," loving the same skirt. Then someone disses her for being blonde, and another boosts her score for it. Talk about confusing, right? Her meter's going nuts, flipping from green to red, up and down. Jane's feeling all kinds of mixed ups and downs – happy one moment and sad the next.

So, think about this wild scene. Can these random opinions about her look really say if Jane's a good person or not? They don't even know her! They're just shouting based on a quick glance.

Who Should Control the Meter?

Why should Jane let her worth be tossed around by other people's random and clashing views? Imagine if she just set that meter to "worthy" herself and didn't let anyone else mess with it. Do you think she'd feel better, more chill, knowing her worth's not up for public debate?

And here's another thing: Why should someone get treated better just 'cause they fit someone else's idea of pretty, smart, or cool? That doesn't make sense, right?

So, Jane's story? It's like a big, flashing neon sign saying, "You define your worth, not anyone else."

Keep your meter set to "worthy," 'cause guess what?

You totally are, no matter what anyone else shouts from the sidelines.

Self-Worth and Love: The Real Deal

Everyone's worthy of love, no exceptions!

Yo, remember this: Every single person is totally worthy of love, no matter how they look. Nobody's opinion has the power to decide if you're lovable or not.

Think about it: People dig different things. One person might be all about ginger cats, while another is team white cat all the way. What one person's not into, someone else might totally adore.

And get this: Even peeps who've made big mistakes or seem 'unworthy' (like criminals or those history book villains) can find love. It's all about realizing that one person's view doesn't define how lovable you are.

Love isn't a perfection contest.

Love's not about hitting some high score on a 'perfect part-ner' scale. It's about finding someone who gets you, loves you for you – quirks, curves, and all.

"I FEEL I'M NOT GOOD ENOUGH THE WAY I AM"

So, picture this: You're in this beautiful flower garden, right? And each flower in this garden is like a person in the world. Some flowers pop open super early, while others take their sweet time. You've got tall flowers, short ones, some rocking bright colors, and others with chill, low-key vibes. Each flower, just by being itself, makes the garden this amazing, diverse place.

Now, think about you as one of these flowers. Just by being you – with your own style, your own pace, and your own color – you're adding something special to the world's garden.

This garden? It's a lot like humanity. Each person, including you, is enough just by being themselves. You don't need to be taller, brighter, or anything else – you're perfect for your spot in the garden, adding your own unique kind of awesome.

In humanity's garden, everyone fits in.

ROLE-PLAY GAME: HELPING EMMA FEEL LOVED

Imagine you have a friend called Emma. She's super sweet, always there for you, great at keeping secrets, encourages you and makes you feel really happy. Like a really great friend. But now this guy she's into called her a 'fat cow,' and now she's feeling like no one will ever love her. She says, "I'm too overweight to be loved."

Your mission? Lift her spirits with some truth bombs about love and worth.

Questions to Ponder and How to Reply

1. Can One Person Decide Emma's Lovability?
Your Reply: _____
Jane's Reply: No way! Everyone's got their own taste. Just 'cause one dude's not into her doesn't mean someone else won't think she's amazing.

2. Why Could Emma Still Find Love?
Your Reply: _____
Jane's Reply: There are so many peeps out there, and someone's bound to dig Emma just as she is. Plus, she's a super nice person.

3. What Rocks About Emma's Friendship?
Your Reply: _____
Jane's Reply: Her personality, for sure! She's the kind of friend who makes life brighter, no matter what she looks like.

4. Team Emma or Team Lara?
Lara is this really beautiful skinny girl. But her personality is like a snake covered in thorns. She's all about finding

faults, insulting people, and sharing their secrets to hurt them.

So, whom would you rather be friends with? Beauty queen Lara or kind Emma?

Your Reply: _____

Jane's Reply: 100% Team Emma. Being nice and real matters way more than just looks.

5. Could a BF Dig Emma's Awesome Traits?

Your Reply: _____

Jane's Reply: Emma, you're totally lovable! You're this amazing person who deserves all the love.

Boosting Emma's Confidence

Emma: "I'm not worthy of love."

You: _____

By reflecting on Emma's situation, we get to see how our own views on worth and love shape our world. It's about understanding that worthiness isn't skin deep – it's about who we are on the inside.

BELIEF CHECK: "I FEEL LIKE EVERYTHING'S ALWAYS MY FAULT!"

Imagine you're part of a dance duo. It's all about moving together, right? But let's say your dance partner steps on your toes. Ouch! And then they blame you!

Is it only your fault for having your toes stepped on? Doesn't quite sound fair, does it? They stepped on you, and then they're blaming you!

In the 'dance' of a relationship, both partners play their parts. If something goes offbeat, it's not just on one person. Blaming your- self all the time? That's like saying you're responsible for every misstep, even the ones you didn't make.

In the dance of relationships, it's about teamwork, not solo guilt trips.

If someone's trying to blame it all on you every time, that's toxic, and you totally don't have to accept it.

Just because someone says it's your fault doesn't mean it actually is!

BUILDING YOUR TREASURE TROVE

The best way to feel better about yourself is to remember all the little things that make you awesome. Take out a journal or note- book and write answers to these questions:

1. When was a time you felt really good about yourself? Describe it.
   1. List 3 good things about yourself. It could be your hair, your nose, or some positive parts of your personality.

2. List 5 times you did something really well. It could be an exam you aced, a contest you won, a new hobby you mastered, or a great idea you got. Something that made you feel happy, proud, special, smart, cool, or unique. For instance, Jane remembers having climbed a very high wall. Liz remembers the first time she managed to ride a horse. Ron remembers how awesome it felt to learn to ski and rocket down the mountainside faster than all his friends.

3. Beneath your 5 good memories, write down what that means about you. For instance, if you overcame something really difficult, that means you're resilient, strong, and a winner. To figure out what it means about you, think "winning the game means I am...". Your Thought could be "a winner, strong, capable, driven, focused, a great player..."

Then phrase it as an affirmation: "I am a winner." "I am capable." "I am strong." "People like me." Stuff like that.

The next time someone tells you that you're a loser, remember the time you succeeded and tell yourself "I am a winner, and I can win again."

4

GUILT TRIPS

A guilt trip is when someone makes you feel guilty for not doing what they want. For instance, they might say you're selfish for doing the things you want, like hanging out with friends instead of being there for them all the time. The truth is this is just a cheap manipulation. To not let them drag you along on their fake guilt trip, here are some affirmations to help you strengthen your self-esteem and self-respect.

AFFIRMATIONS TO COUNTER GUILT TRIPS

- **I have the right to my own time and space.**
- **Choosing for myself doesn't make me selfish or ungrateful.**
- **I am not responsible for others' happiness.**

- My feelings and needs are just as important as anyone else's.
- Saying 'no' does not make me a bad person or partner.
- I deserve to pursue my own interests and hobbies.
- I am worthy of respect and understanding.
- My value isn't measured by how much I sacrifice for others.
- I choose to act out of love, not guilt.
- I am strong enough to resist manipulation and stand by my choices.
- It's okay for me to do the things I want, just like it's okay for others to do what they want.
- I let others live their lives the way they want. And I deserve to be treated the same way.
- It's okay for me to have my own life and to live it the way that I want.

MENTAL PROMPT EXERCISE TO RECLAIM YOUR POWER

Reflect on these questions:

1. Think of a time you felt guilt-tripped. What was the situation? How did you react?
2. What are some things you enjoy doing for yourself that others have made you feel guilty about?

Mentally recall why it's totally okay for you to do those things and why you're still a good person.

3. How do you feel when you do things out of guilt? (Spoiler: Any time you feel bad, that's a sign of something being seriously off. It's like an inner compass that's screaming "TOXIC!")

4. Reflect on how you can balance your own needs with your relationships.

5. Remind yourself daily that your needs and wants are valid. Start with "My wants and needs..."

AFFIRMATIONS TO CLAIM YOUR INDEPENDENCE

Remember, you're an awesome original, not a copy. These affirmations are here to remind you of that. Say them, believe them, live them!

1. "My style is my signature."
Rock those clothes, that hair, that look. It's your style, and it's amazing.

2. "My hobbies and passions are my playground."
Whether it's gaming, painting, or playing guitar, your hobbies are all about you being you.

3."My feelings are valid, always."
Happy, sad, excited, or mad – your feelings are real and totally yours.

4. "My thoughts are my power."
Your ideas and opinions? They're valuable and worth sharing.

5. "My wants and needs matter."
What you want and need is important – from the food you love to the dreams you chase.

6. "I am in charge of my happiness."
Your joy is yours to create and cherish, no one else's.

7. "My voice is unique and deserves to be heard."
Speak up, speak out. Your voice adds to the world's melody.

8. "I am the author of my story. I am in control of my life. I am in control of my future."
Write your chapters and choose your adventures. It's your life story.

9. "I am enough, just as I am."
No 'ifs,' 'buts,' or 'shoulds.' You're perfectly you, and that's more than enough.

10. "I choose my path and walk it with confidence."
Your journey, your steps. Walk them with your head held high.

Every time you feel like someone's trying to dim your shine or change your tune, remember these affirmations and say them to yourself (even quietly). You're the boss of your world, your choices, your life. Don't let anyone tell you otherwise. You're a star, and stars are meant to shine bright, in their own way.

So, go out there and be unapologetically you. Your independence – your uniqueness – is your superpower. Embrace it, celebrate it, and own it. You got this!

MENTAL EXERCISE: CELEBRATE UNIQUENESS

Exploring the Fame of Being Unique

1. **Pick 3 Celebs with a Unique Vibe:** Think of three famous people who totally stand out because of their style, talents, music, or even their looks. Commit them to memory.

2. **How Did Their Uniqueness Rock Their World?** Give some thought to how their unique qualities helped them become rich, famous, loved, or popular. Did their one-of-a-kind style make them a household name? Did their unusual talent skyrocket them to fame?

Deep Dive Questions:

- **Q1) What If They Were 'Normal'?** Imagine if these celebs had ditched their uniqueness and gone for a regular life. Like, what if Rihanna had become a secretary instead of a music icon? How different would her life be? Would she still be the beloved star she is today?

- **Q2) Why Being Unique is Awesome**: Why do you think being different is a good thing? What makes standing out from the crowd something to celebrate?

- **Q3) What are some benefits of being unique?** What 'good' can come out of it? Consider 3 positive things that happened to unique people.

Recognizing Your Own Unique Superpowers:

Now, think about what makes YOU special. Mentally note three things that make you uniquely awesome. Maybe it's your chill vibe, a hidden talent, or your quirky sense of style.

Try continuing these sentences:

"I have a unique..." "My... is unique..." "I have a great..."

Turning 'Flaws' into Wins:

Next, consider three things you think are 'not-so-great' unique traits about yourself. Now, flip the script! How can these traits be seen as positives? Like, if you have super sensitive hearing, your friends might give you a hard time and maybe you feel bad because you can't attend loud rock concerts. But hey, those ears are unique! Maybe you're a natural for a career in music production or sound engineering.

How do your unique traits help you right now? Maybe your keen hearing lets you enjoy music on a deeper level or makes you the family's official "car-approaching" alert system.

Get creative and think of some wild, fun ways your uniqueness could shape your future. Could your love for detailed doodling make you a sought-after graphic designer? Your knack for remembering random facts make you a quiz show champ?

Wrapping Up: Embracing Your Uniqueness

Your uniqueness is your superpower, and this exercise is all about embracing it. Whether it's something that makes you stand out or a trait you're learning to love, it's all part of what makes you, well, you! So keep celebrating your unique self, and who knows where your special qualities will take you!

Remember, in the grand story of life, your uniqueness is your signature. It's what makes your chapter so exciting and unforgettable. Keep writing your story, one unique trait at a time. You're amazing just the way you are!

JOURNALING EXERCISE: 3 GOOD THINGS ABOUT YOU

Write down 3 special unique things about yourself. These could be your kind personality, a special skill or a talent, or even just how you look. Remember, some people became famous and rich just because of their looks – including 'unusual' looks.

SPREAD KINDNESS LIKE CONFETTI

"Kindness is a language which the deaf can hear and the blind can see."

— MARK TWAIN

Ever heard the saying, "What goes around, comes around"? Well, it's time to sprinkle some kindness and watch it grow into something beautiful. Here's a little secret: doing good for others doesn't just help them; it gives you a happiness boost, too!

Now, I've got a tiny but mighty favor to ask you...

Would you be willing to light up someone's world, someone you might not even know? Imagine them a bit like your younger self: eager to grow, hoping for change, and searching for a guiding light but not quite sure where to find it.

Our hearts and soul are poured into making recovery from toxic relationships a beacon of hope for everyone. Our dream? To spread this message far and wide. But we've got a small challenge: reaching every single person who needs this guide.

And here's where you, yes YOU, come in. Believe it or not, your voice is powerful. A lot of folks decide on a book based on what others say about it. So, on behalf of a teen navigating through a toxic relationship somewhere out there:

Your mission, should you choose to accept, is to share your thoughts on this book.

This isn't about spending money. It's about donating a few moments of your time, which could forever alter the course of another teen's life. Your review has the magic to:

- ...help one more person feel understood and less alone.
- ...support someone in finding the courage to seek healthier relationships.
- ...offer a lifeline to those drowning in doubt and confusion.
- ...inspire another soul to reclaim their confidence and happiness.
- ...turn someone's life story from despair to hope.

Feeling that warm glow inside already? To make your act of kind- ness a reality (in under a minute!), here's what to do: leave a heartfelt review.

Just zap the QR code right here:

https://www.amazon.com/review/create-review/?ie=UTF8&channel=glance-detail&asin=

If the thought of helping a struggling teen out there makes your heart happy, you're definitely our kind of superhero. Welcome to the squad!

I'm super thrilled to embark on this journey with you toward a Toxic-Free Life with more confidence than you ever imag- ined. You're gonna be wowed by the guidance and insight waiting for you in the chapters ahead.

A million thanks for being awesome. Let's dive back into trans- forming lives together.

- Your cheerleader,

Jordan Phoenix

5

LIES AND MANIPULATIONS

UNRAVELING THE DANGEROUS WEB OF 'FALSE TRUTHS'

Ever notice how, sometimes, a small bit of truth gets twisted into a big, hurtful lie? That's what we call 'false truths.' It's like someone takes one tiny thing and blows it up into a full-on attack on who you are.

How They Generalize and Hurt

The Ugly Hairdo Becomes "You're Ugly": Say you try a new hairdo, and someone doesn't like it. Instead of just dissing the hairstyle, they go all, "You look ugly." Bam! Suddenly, it's not about the hair; it's about you as a person. **One Lost Game Turns Into "You're a Loser"**: You lose a sports match, and someone's like, "You're such a loser." Ouch. It's not just the game you lost; now it feels like your whole identity is being called a 'loser.'

The Harmful Impact

These kinds of insults can really mess with your head. You start thinking, "Am I really a failure or ugly?" Your self-esteem takes a hit, and your confidence? Down the drain. It's like wearing glasses that make everything about you look bad.

Sometimes, in a relationship, one person tries to play this twisted game where they use 'false truths' to make you feel small. Let's talk about Derek and his GF as an example.

Derek's Story: The Eiffel Tower Trap

Derek's GF is like a walking trivia game. She knows all sorts of random facts, like how fast a llama can sprint or the number of stairs in the Eiffel Tower. Cool, right? But here's the catch: She uses this knowledge to put Derek down. When Derek can't answer her trivia questions, she's all, "You don't know how many stairs the Eiffel Tower has? You're a stupid idiot! You don't know anything!"

The Half-Truth Hook

See, she's hooking him with a half-truth. Yeah, Derek doesn't know some random fact, but does that make him stupid? Heck no! But because there's a tiny bit of truth in what she says (the part about not knowing the number of stairs),

Derek starts to believe the whole thing, including the 'stupid idiot' part.

Breaking Down the 'False Truth' Technique

This is where we need to get our detective hats on and do some critical thinking. Just because one part of a statement is true doesn't make the whole thing true. It's like a sandwich with a slice of truth and a whole lot of nonsense.

Critical Thinking to the Rescue

So, here's how to break it down:

Acknowledge the Fact: "Okay, so I don't know the number of stairs. True."

Challenge the Insult: "But hey, not knowing that doesn't make me stupid. I know tons of other cool stuff!"

Remember, your intelligence isn't measured by trivia, not knowing something someone asks, or measuring yourself against others. It's about how you think, learn, and see the world. Not knowing one thing doesn't erase all the awesome stuff you do know.

Flipping the Script: Own Your Knowledge

The next time someone tries to pull a 'Derek's GF' on you, remember: what you don't know doesn't define you. You're smart in your own way, and not knowing one thing doesn't change who you are.

By understanding the trick of 'false truths,' you can start to see when someone's trying to manipulate you with half-baked statements. Stick to your guns, and remember, your worth isn't a quiz score. You're way more than that. Stay sharp, stay you!

Beliefs Shaping Actions

Our beliefs drive what we do and how we react. When you start buying into these false truths, like thinking you're unworthy or not good enough, it can change the whole course of your life. You might hold back from going after what you want, feel like you don't deserve good stuff, or worse, believe you deserve the bad stuff.

The Example of Jenny

Take Jenny, for example. She failed an exam, and someone told her, "You're so stupid." Since 'being stupid' seemed like a 'logical' reason, she believed it. Now, she's scared to speak up, try new things, or chase her dreams. It's like one false belief put up a bunch of roadblocks in her life.

Abusers' Manipulative Tactics

Abusers are pros at this game. They use these false truths to make their victims feel small, unworthy, and at fault. It's a way to keep control. If you believe you're the problem, you're less likely to stand up for yourself or think you deserve better.

It's the main reason why people let their partner hurt them, insult them, hit them, and even sexually abuse them – because they think they deserve it!

The Danger of Accepting False Truths

These false truths, because they seem to make sense at first, can trap you in a cycle of negative thinking. You start accepting the abuse, blaming yourself, feeling guilty, and thinking you're not worthy of anything better. It's like living in a world where every mirror shows a distorted version of you.

But here's the thing: Just because someone says it doesn't make it true. You're not what they say you are. You're way more than a failed test, a lost game, or a hairstyle. You're a whole person with a ton of worth, and no one's flawed opinion can change that.

Remember, you have the power to challenge these false truths. Don't let someone else's words dictate your worth. You're worthy, you're enough, and you definitely deserve a life filled with love and respect. Stay strong and trust in your own truth.

EXAMPLES

The "Always Wrong" Trap

Alex and Sam are chillin' together, and Sam's talking about her favorite band. Out of nowhere, Alex goes, "You got the song title wrong. You always get things wrong." Sam starts to feel like maybe she's not that smart after all.

Typical Sentences:

- "You're always messing up. Can't you get anything right?"
- "Seriously, Sam? That's not how it happened. Do you ever remember things correctly?"
- "That's not the right artist, Sam. You mix them up every time. How do you not know this by now?"
- "No, Sam, you've got it all wrong _again_! It's like talking to a wall. How do you always manage to remember things so inaccurately?"

The "Never Good Enough" Game

Bella tries her best to look nice for her date with Jordan. But when she shows up, Jordan smirks, "You're wearing that? You never look as good as other girls." Bella's confidence starts to crumble, feeling she'll never be pretty enough.

Typical Sentences:

- "Why can't you look more like [Jasmine]? You never dress well."
- "Is that your choice for tonight? You always seem to miss the mark compared to others like Cindy!"
- "You went with that hairstyle? It's like you're not

even trying to stand out. You never do shine quite like the rest."

The "Constant Comparison" Con

Every time Mike and his GF, Leah, hang out, she compares him to her ex, saying things like, "My ex would have known how to fix this. You're just clueless." Mike begins to doubt his abilities, feeling inferior.

Typical Sentences:

- "My ex was so much better at this than you. You just don't measure up."
- "Honestly, my ex would have had this sorted in minutes. It's not that hard."
- "Why can't you be more like her? She would have done it perfectly."

The "Love With Conditions" Lie

Emma's BF, Tyler, often says, "If you really loved me, you'd do this for me." So, Emma bends over backward, trying to prove her love, fearing that she's not loving enough as she is.

Typical Sentences:

- "If you really loved me, you wouldn't argue. You'd just do what I say."

- Remember, if you truly cared about us, you'd make this sacrifice. Love is about doing things you don't always want to do.

The "Isolation Tactic" Twist

Whenever Hannah wants to hang with friends, her BF, Chris, guilts her, saying, "You'd rather be with them than me. Guess I'm not important." Hannah starts to feel guilty for having a life outside of him.

Typical Sentence:

- "You always choose others over me. I guess I'm just not that important to you."
- "Oh, going out again? It's like you live a whole other life without me. Makes me wonder where I stand."
- "Must be nice to have fun without me. It's clear where your priorities lie, and it's obviously not with us."

Remember, these 'false truths' are nothing more than manipulation tactics. They're designed to make you doubt yourself and feel reliant on the abuser. It's important to recognize them for what they are – tools of control, not reflections of your true worth. You're way more than these twisted words. Stay aware and stay strong!

EVIL BRAIN TRICKS DECODED

Did you know that those sneaky manipulative tricks, the 'false truths,' are super common in not-so-great relationships? So common, in fact, that experts have studied them and given them fancy names! It's like they're the go-to weapons for people looking to control or put others down.

When someone's throwing these false truths at you, remember, it's not you that's the problem. It's them using these well-known, manipulative strategies. They're like relationship clichés, used by people all over the world to play mind games.

Now let's dive into some high-level stuff. We're talking about some university-level brain gymnastics here, so if you get this, you're basically a genius!

We're about to expose 'false truths' (or as experts call them, 'logical fallacies') used in manipulative relationships.

Understanding these is like having a secret decoder for when someone's trying to mess with you. It will help you see clearly when something is NOT true so you don't fall for these fake truths. Trust me, it will save you a lot of heartache.

Next time someone tries to hit you with one of these, you can totally flip the script. Imagine them saying something mean, and you spin around, all cool and collected, and hit them with, "Nice try, but that's just an 'Ad Hominem' fallacy. You're trying to make me feel bad and control me. Not cool.

I'm not [whatever they said]." Watch their jaws drop when you call out their game with those fancy terms. It's like having a secret superpower in the world of words.

So, now you're not just defending yourself; you're schooling them in psychology and logic. How awesome is that? Keep this knowledge in your back pocket, and remember, you're way smarter than their mind tricks.

The List of 'False Truths' (aka Fallacies) Used to Manipulate and Control:

1. **The 'You're Just...' Attack** (Ad Hominem Fallacy):

   - When they attack you instead of the topic or problem. Like, "You're just too stupid to get what I mean." "You're too young to understand" "You're a boy, of course you wouldn't get it."

2. **The 'If You Loved Me' Trick** (Emotional Appeal Fallacy):

   - Emotional blackmail alert! "If you really loved me, you wouldn't do what I want."
   - Love doesn't have conditions. You can show your love in many ways. You don't have to do XYZ to prove your love.

FROM PAIN TO EMPOWERMENT: | 325

3. **The 'You're Saying I...' Misfire** (Straw Man Fallacy):

- Twisting your words. "You want some alone time? So, you're saying you don't want to be with me?"
- Wanting time alone is one thing, not wanting to be with you is completely separate. Twisting them together is manipulation (trying to get you to not spend any time alone but just be together all the time).

4. **The 'One Thing Leads to Disaster' Slide** (Slippery Slope Fallacy):

- Overreacting to small things and thinking one little thing will lead to a bigger thing. "Going out with friends tonight? Next thing, you won't be seeing me at all! Guess our relationship is over."
- Come on! Going out with her friends doesn't mean she won't have time for him ever again.

5. **The 'This or That' Trap** (False Dichotomy):

- Only two extreme choices. "Either we move in together now, or we break up."
- That's manipulation. There are always other choices and ways to meet both of your wants and needs.

6. **The 'After All I've Done' Guilt Trip** (Guilt-Tripping):

- "After everything I've done for you, you can't do this one thing?"
- You never have to do anything you don't want to do, even if your bae did XYZ for you.

7. **The 'It's Your Fault I'm Mad' Blame Shift** (Victim Blaming):

- Shifting the blame for their wrong actions onto you. "You make me angry because you're always messing up." "It's your fault I'm angry, you shouldn't have worn that dress!" Never true! Their actions, their words, their anger – that's on them.

8. **The 'Never Good Enough'** (Goalpost Move):

- Changing what they want after you've done it. "You got a job, but not the one I wanted." "You won the game, but not fast enough." "You got an A, but you didn't win an award." And so on.

9. **The 'I'm Right Because I'm Right' Circle** (Circular Reasoning Fallacy):

- "I'm right because I say I'm right." Uh, nope. You saying you're right doesn't make you right.

10. **The 'Everyone's Doing It'** (Bandwagon Fallacy):

- "All my friends do that, so you should too." Just because others do it doesn't mean it's the right thing for you to do. Your feelings and opinions matter and should be respected.

11. **The 'I'm Older, So I Know Better'** (Appeal to Authority Fallacy):

- "I'm older, so obviously, I know better about this." Being older does NOT mean they know better or that your opinion doesn't matter.
- It can also come in a sneaky way of showing you someone famous or cool who did what they want you to do and then trying to get you to do the same thing. "Jenny is a famous actress and Jenny did it, so you should too."

Why Knowing This Stuff Matters

Recognizing these 'false truths' is like unlocking a secret level in the game of relationships. It helps you see when someone's trying to play mind games. Remember, in a healthy relationship, it's all about respect, honesty, and understanding – not these sneaky mind tricks.

You've got the power to spot these tricks and call them out. Keep your eyes open and trust your gut. You're smarter than these false truths, and you deserve real, honest love.

OVERCOMING 'FALSE TRUTHS': YOUR REFLECTIVE EXERCISE

Seeing Through the Fog of Words

Ever had someone say something to you that just felt off? Like, they say something hurtful, but they twist it so it sounds almost true? It's like they're using some weird logic to make you feel bad or doubt yourself. Well, it's time to put on your detective hat and see through these 'false truths.' Let's get started!

Step-by-Step Instructions:

1. **Recall the Experience**: Think back to a recent time when someone said something that left you feeling confused, insulted, or just plain bad about yourself.

2. **Write Down the Words**: Jot down exactly what they said. Try to remember their exact words, no matter how harsh they might seem now.

3. **Their 'Logic'**: What reasons did they give you to back up what they said? Did they try to make it sound like they were just stating facts?

4. **Why You Believed Them**: Reflect on why their words seemed believable at the time. Was it because of who they were or how they said it?

5. **Spot the Fallacies**: Now, put on your critical thinking cap. Can you identify any logical fallacies in their argument? Like, were they making a huge generalization or attacking you instead of the issue?

6. **Another Perspective**: Take a step back and try to see the situation in a new light. Is there a different, more positive way to look at it? Maybe they were projecting their own issues onto you, or maybe they were just plain wrong.

Wrapping Up: Seeing the Truth

By doing this exercise, you're learning to separate hurtful words from reality. You're figuring out how to spot when someone's using twisted logic to bring you down. Remember, just because someone says something doesn't make it true. Trust in your own perception, your own feelings, and your own truth. You got this!

Stay strong, keep questioning, and never forget that your perspective matters. You're more than someone else's words – you're a whole universe of thoughts, feelings, and truths. Keep shining your light!

6

CYBERBULLYING

Cyberbullying can totally wreck your self-esteem and make you feel unloved and depressed. If you're being cyberbullied or were cyberbullied, it's important to take care of your mental health. Repeat positive affirmations, do some fun things you love, and spend time in the real world away from the toxicity online.

POSITIVE AFFIRMATIONS TO COMBAT CYBERBULLYING

When you're dealing with cyberbullying, it's super important to remind yourself of your worth. Here are some affirmations to repeat every day. Say them out loud, write them down, or even set them as your phone wallpaper – whatever works for you!

- "I am more than what others say online." "I am worthy of respect and kindness."
- "I am strong and can overcome negativity."
- "My self-worth isn't defined by others' opinions."
- "I choose to focus on the love and support around me."
- "I am capable of rising above hate."
- "My feelings are valid, and I deserve to be heard."
- "I am loved, and I will not let cyberbullying define me."

POSITIVITY EXERCISE: RECLAIMING YOUR SPACE

Step 1: Digital Detox

Start by taking a little break from social media. It's like hitting the pause button on all that negativity. Use this time to do things that make you feel good – reading, hanging out with friends, drawing, dancing – anything that brings you joy.

Step 2: Gratitude Journaling

Every day, write down three things you're grateful for in your life. It could be anything – your pet, your favorite song, a good laugh with a friend. This helps shift your focus from the negative to the positive.

Step 3: Connect with Supporters

Spend time with people who uplift you. Chat with friends who make you laugh or hang out with family who have your back. It's all about surrounding yourself with positivity.

Step 4: Reflect and Grow

At the end of each day, take a few minutes to reflect on something positive that happened or something you did well. It's about recognizing the good in every day, no matter how small.

Wrapping Up: You're Stronger Than You Know

Remember, cyberbullying can be tough, but you're tougher. These affirmations and exercises are tools to help you rebuild your confidence and keep your head held high. You're amazing, and don't let anyone – especially some online bully – make you think otherwise.

If you need help, go to Cyberbullying.org for advice and support, and talk to an adult you can trust.

7

PHYSICAL ABUSE

Physical abuse is terribly harmful. One of the most important things to address is the feeling victims have that it's all their fault and they somehow deserved it.

Even if you weren't physically abused, but if you were abused in any other way, the following exercises will help you overcome the misplaced deep feeling of guilt and shame.

"IT'S YOUR FAULT I HURT YOU! YOU MADE ME DO IT!"

When They Say It's Your Fault – It's Not!

Ever played a game where you get blamed for stuff that's totally out of your control? Like another character shoots at you, or you fall into a trap that the game developer made, and someone's like, "That's totally your fault! You deserved it!" Crazy, right? Well, that's exactly what happens in some relationships when it comes to reacting to stuff.

In an abusive relationship, your partner might hurt you and then say things like, "You made me do it!" or "If only you hadn't said that, I wouldn't have gotten so mad."

You might feel it's unfair but feel guilty and ashamed anyway.

But here's the thing – *it's never your fault. No one deserves to be hurt, EVER.*

Why It's Not Your Fault:

1. **Choice and Control**: Remember, everyone has a choice in how they react. One person might react in a cool, calm way. Another might react violently. If someone chooses to hurt you, it's on them, not you. Just like in a game, if someone shoots at you, it's their decision, not your fault.

2. **Blame Game**: Abusers often play the blame game to control and manipulate you. It's their way of avoiding responsibility for their actions. It's like a magician using misdirection – they want you to look away from what's really happening.

3. **Understanding the Damage**: Being constantly blamed can mess with your head. It can make you doubt yourself and even believe you're the problem.

But that's the abuser's voice in your head, not the truth. It's like wearing glasses with the wrong prescription – it distorts your view of reality.

The Psychology Behind It

1. **Gaslighting**: This is when someone tries to make you doubt your own experiences and perceptions. Imagine if someone kept changing the rules of a game but insisted they were always the same. Confusing, right?
2. **Self-Doubt**: Constant blame can lead to self-doubt. It's like if you kept losing in a game and started to think maybe you're just bad at it, even if the game was rigged against you.
3. **Fear and Control**: Abusers use blame to create fear and maintain control. It's their way of keeping you in the game, even when it's harming you.

Breaking Free from Blame

1. **Affirm Your Reality**: Keep a journal or talk to trusted friends about what's happening. It's like keeping a scorecard – it helps you see the game for what it really is.
2. **Seek Support**: Talk to someone who understands, like a counselor or a support group. It's like getting a guide for a really tough game.

3. **Affirmations**: Practice telling yourself the truth – that you're worthy, you're capable, and you don't deserve to be treated badly. It's like giving yourself a pep talk before a big game.

4. **Understand Your Worth**: Remember, you're valuable and deserving of respect. Just like in a game, you're the main character in your life – don't let someone else control your story.

Conclusion: Your Strength and Your Future

Realizing and accepting that the abuse and the blame aren't your fault is like leveling up in understanding yourself. It takes strength, but you've got it. You have the power to step out of the horror game and into a new reality where you're respected, loved, and safe.

Remember, in the story of your life, you're the hero – and heroes deserve happy endings.

DIFFERENT REACTIONS: IT'S ALL ABOUT CHOICES

Picture this: Your friend totally bombs a test. Here's how different peeps might react:

1. **Healthy Reaction**: One friend goes, "Bummer, man. Let's study together next time." That's a chill, supportive vibe.

2. **Unhealthy Reaction**: Her boyfriend flips out, "Bitch, you're so dumb! You're a total loser!" And he slaps her. That's just harsh, abusive, and totally not cool.

Or imagine you're rocking a new outfit that you think is fire, but your BF/GF isn't into it. Check out these reactions:

1. **Healthy Reaction**: They might be like, "Not my style, but you do you!"
2. See, that's respecting your choice.
3. **Unhealthy Reaction**: Or they go all, "You can't wear that! Change now! Or I'll punch you!" That's controlling, abusive, and a major red flag.

Freedom to Choose = Responsibility

Everyone's got the freedom to choose how they react. If your BF/GF chooses to get angry or upset over small stuff or even big stuff – that's on them, not you.

Like, say you can't hang out 'cause you gotta study or chill with your squad.

Here's how it can go down:

4. **Healthy Reaction**: They're like, "Cool, catch you later!" That's understanding and respecting your space.
   1. **Unhealthy Reaction**: But if they throw a fit, like

"You never spend time with me!" – that's manipulative.

2. Or worse, they punch you or kick you and then say it's your fault because you wanted to hang with your friends. That's abusive and toxic!

The Bottom Line: Their Reaction, Their Responsibility

So, here's the deal: how someone reacts is their choice, and it says more about them than about you. If they choose to be under- standing and cool, that's awesome. But if they choose to be controlling or mean, that's on them, and it's not cool.

It's like in a game – if you make a move and someone else freaks out, it's their issue, not yours. You're not responsible for how they choose to react.

Remember, in a healthy relationship, peeps respect each other's choices and reactions. It's about supporting, not controlling. So, next time someone tries to blame you for their reaction,

remember, it's their choice, and you don't have to own it. Stay true to you, and don't let anyone mess with your vibe!

WHY IT'S NOT YOUR FAULT

When someone decides to hurt you, it's on them, not you. Let's break it down, teen style:

1. Agency and Choice

Everyone's got their own mind, right? We all make choices based on what we think and believe. So, when someone chooses to hurt you, that's all on them. It's like choosing between a chocolate or vanilla ice cream – it's their pick, based on their taste (or, in this case, their character).

2. Cause and Effect Misinterpretation

Ever been told, "You made me do it"? Nah, that's not how it works. Just because you disagreed or asked a question doesn't mean you caused their hurtful behavior. Their reaction (like getting mad or violent) comes from their own issues, not because of what you did or said.

3. Stimulus and Response

Picture this: You say you like a different band than your friend does. That's the stimulus. If they start yelling at you, that's their choice of response. A chill person might just say, "Cool, different tastes."

The way they respond says a lot about them, not about the band or you.

Everyone reacts differently to a stimulus (like you stating you like Taylor Swift while they like Lady Gaga). You are never responsible for their reaction; therefore, their reaction is not your fault.

Understanding Behavior and Character

1. Behavior Reflects the Person

Ever notice how some people are always chill while others lose their cool over small stuff? That's because people's actions show who they are inside. If someone's always aggressive or mean, it's more about their own issues and less about the people they're mean to.

2. Blame-Shifting: Their Defense Mechanism

When someone's like, "You made me do this," they're actually trying to dodge facing their own problems. It's easier for them to point fingers at you than to admit they've got stuff to work on.

3. Healthy vs. Unhealthy Reactions

Here's the thing: Different people react differently to the same stuff. If one person gets violent over a disagreement while another person stays cool, it shows who they are, not what the disagreement was about. It's like two gamers playing the same tough level – one might rage-quit, and the other keeps trying calmly. The game's the same; the players are different.

It's Their Character, Not Your Fault So, bottom line: When someone hurts you, remember that it's their choice and a reflection of who they are. You're not to blame for their actions, and you definitely don't deserve to be treated badly. Stay true to yourself, and don't let anyone's bad vibes change who you are. You're awesome just the way you are!

1. Personal Boundaries

You know how in video games, every character has their own space, their own moves? That's like personal boundaries in real life. You're in charge of your space – your actions, your feelings. But here's the deal: you can't control how others play their game. If someone decides to go rogue, that's on them, not you. Your job? Just keep playing your game the best you can.

2. Self-Compassion

Imagine giving yourself a high-five or a hug every day. That's self-compassion. It's about being your own BFF, understanding that you're not the one messing up when someone else is being mean or hurtful. You deserve to be treated with respect and kindness, no matter what. So next time you're feeling down, remember to treat yourself like you would your best friend.

3. Seeking Healthy Relationships

Let's talk healthy relationships. They're like a perfect playlist – every song complements the other, no track trying to overpower the rest. In a healthy relationship, it's cool to have different opinions, and it doesn't turn into a big drama. It's about mutual respect, where both of you get to be your awesome selves without fear of being put down.

So, you like TayTay while he likes Lady Gaga? That's fine! No need to get angry or violent about that.

Wrapping it Up

Understanding all this stuff is kinda like leveling up in life. It's realizing that if someone chooses to be hurtful, it's a reflection of them, not you. You've got to remember, you're not the game controller for someone else's actions. This understanding is huge – it's the start of healing, seeing yourself in a new light, and moving towards the kind of relationship where you're treated like the rockstar you are. Remember, you're awesome just the way you are, and no one has the right to make you feel otherwise!

REFLECTIVE EXERCISES:

The Tale of Two Dogs and a Girl Named Anna

Imagine this: There are two dogs. One's a Rottweiler, a tough- looking dude who's had it rough. He's from a shelter, and in his past life, he was beaten up. Like, whenever his old owner raised a hand, it wasn't for pets, but for hits, especially on his head. Not cool, right?

Then, there's this brown poodle, the chill type. He comes from a super peaceful home where he was treated like a king. Lots of head pats, cuddles, and no shouting or hitting. He's totally into getting his head pet.

So, here comes Anna, this young girl who loves dogs. She goes to pet the Rottweiler, right? But the moment she reaches out, the guy freaks and bites her hand. Ouch!

Next up, Anna tries petting the poodle. And guess what? He's all about it. He licks her hand, wags his tail, and is just living for those head pats.

The Big Questions

Now, think about it: Why did these two dogs react so differently? Anna's the same person with both. She's just being herself, but each dog gives her a totally different reaction.

Is it something Anna did? Or is it more about how each dog's been treated in the past, shaping how they react now?

Do their reactions say anything about Anna being a good or bad person?

And hey, what about the Rottweiler biting Anna? Is that on her? Is she a bad person because he reacted that way?

Or is the bite more about the Rottweiler's past and his choice to react that way?

Contemplate Your Thoughts:

_____

_____

_____

_____

_____

Reflecting on the Story

The truth is, it's not Anna's fault the Rottweiler bit her. It was his choice and his action. That's totally on him, it's his fault.

This story is like a mirror, showing us how past experiences shape reactions.

It's a reminder that sometimes, how someone reacts to us has more to do with their past and less with what we're doing in the present.

So, what do you think about Anna's situation?

Remember, like with Anna and the dogs, how people react to us can be about their history, their fears, and their choices. It's not always about what we did or didn't do. Understanding this can help us see things from a different angle and be more empathetic to others and to ourselves. Stay thoughtful and keep an open heart!

The Tale of Two Step-Brothers and a Puppy

Picture this: Two step-brothers, Ron and Joe. They're like night and day. Ron's got this aggressive, angry vibe. Joe, on the other hand, is chill, kind, and all about spreading love.

Their dad brings home this adorable puppy, Roofus. He's all wiggly, happy, and loves to play. When Roofus wants attention, he does what pups do best – he barks!

Different Reactions to the Same Bark

So, here's the deal. When Roofus barks at Ron, especially when Ron's trying to focus on homework, Ron flips out. He's like, "Bad dog! Be quiet! You're messing up my study time!" Ron sees the barking as a huge no-no. He gets super mad and even hits Roofus.

But check out how Joe handles it. When Roofus barks at him, even if Joe's super busy with homework, he's all calm and understanding. He's like, "Not now, Roofus, I gotta study, buddy. Shhh!" If Roofus keeps it up, Joe might toss him a toy or give him a quick pat before getting back to his books. Joe never gets mad at Roofus. He's all about the cuddles and love.

Thinking Cap Time: Why the Difference?

So, why do Ron and Joe react so differently to the same thing – Roofus barking? Is it because they're just wired differently, each with their own way of dealing with stuff? Or did Roofus somehow make them act like this?

Your Thought: _____

And how about this: Ron says it's Roofus's fault he hit him.

But could Roofus really make Ron and Joe behave so differently? Who's actually responsible for how Ron and Joe react – and why?

Your Thought: _____

Now, who 'made' Ron be harsh with Roofus, and who 'made' Joe treat Roofus kindly?

If you think no one 'made' them act that way, why do you think they did what they did?

Your Thought: _____

Wrapping Up: Understanding Reactions

This story shows us that how people react to the same situation can be totally different. It's about their character, their mindset, and their choice – not about the puppy's actions. Remember, just like Ron and Joe, people choose their reactions, and it's not the puppy's (or anyone else's) fault.

The truth is, even though Ron said, "I hit him because he made me! It's his fault! He barked," it isn't Roofus's fault. It's Ron's choice of how to react to that behavior of barking.

No one can control anyone else's actions. Roofus didn't "make him do it."

Ron behaved that way because he chose to, just like Joe chose to behave in a kind way. It's not Roofus's fault.

In the same way, no matter what 'wrong' thing you may have done, if someone is mean to you, that's their choice, and it's never your fault. There are many other ways to handle a mistake or a 'wrong action,' just like Joe did! It doesn't have to be mean, violent, or hurtful. Remember, everyone makes mistakes, and that's not a sin.

You deserve to be treated with respect, kindness, and love – always.

Affirm: *How someone behaves is their choice, not my fault. I am only responsible for my own actions, and others are only responsible for theirs.*

JOURNALING EXERCISE: TACKLING SELF-BLAME LIKE A BOSS

Hey there! It's time to dive into some real talk with yourself. Grab your journal, find a comfy spot, and let's get those thoughts flowing. These questions are all about helping you see things clearer and ditch any unnecessary self-blame. Ready? Let's roll!

1. Reacting to Your Actions: Think Squad Style: Ever noticed how different your friends, relations, or adults react differently to the same stuff you do?

Like, one friend laughs off a silly mistake, but another might get all moody about it. One relation is cool about something you did, while the other thinks it's terrible. Reflect on this: when you had a disagreement or goofed up, how did different people react?

Write down their different responses from positive to negative.

Why did each of them react differently? Mention their personalities beneath their reactions.

2. Choices, Choices – It's All You: Remember a time when you had to respond to someone else's drama or actions? Did you weigh your options on how to react? What made you decide how to respond?

This is about getting how we all have choices, including those peeps who might be blaming you for their stuff.

3. Spot the Blame Game: Ever been blamed for someone else losing their cool or doing something wrong? Look back at that. Could they have reacted another way? What would've been a more chill and positive reaction from them?

4. You're Not the Puppet Master: Think about a time you felt like it was your fault someone else acted badly. Were you really pulling their strings? If you had a magical remote control for their actions, how would you have made them act? This is about seeing the difference between feeling like it's your fault and actually control- ling someone else's moves.

5. Controlling Their Reactions – Myth or Reality? Think about it: if you really could control their reactions, could you make them do silly stuff like singing a love song or dancing on one foot right now? If you can't make them do these things, it means you don't control their actions, not even the hurtful ones. What does this say about the idea that you're responsible for their behavior?

6. Emotional Influence Check: Remember a time when you reacted intensely to something someone did. What were you feeling at that moment? How did your emotions steer your reaction? This might give you a clue about how others react based on their feelings, not because of what you do.

7. Journey of Personal Growth: How have you changed in dealing with conflicts or disagreements? What influenced these changes in you? Think about this: if your responses have evolved, doesn't it show that how we act is a choice shaped by our growth and who we are as people?

8. Spotting a Healthy Relationship: Reflect on the healthiest relationship you've seen or been a part of. How are disagreements handled there? What does this tell you about the importance of respect and understanding?

9. Dealing with False Accusations: Think back to a time when someone blamed you for something you didn't do. Did their words change the actual truth of the situation?

10. Why the Blame Game? Ever wonder why some peeps are quick to point fingers instead of owning up to their stuff? Think about why it's easier for some to blame others than to take responsibility. Getting this can be a game-changer in shaking off any blame they try to stick on you.

11. Rewind and Reframe: Remember a time when someone tried to make their bad choices your fault? Now, with all you know about personal responsibility, how would you see that situation differently? It's like editing a movie scene with new insights, giving it a whole new meaning.

As you write, remember, the goal is to realize that everyone's responsible for their own actions. You're not to blame for how someone chooses to react, even if they try to make you think so. These prompts are here to help you see that, so take your time, think it through, and let's start turning those pages into a new chapter of understanding and self-compassion.

By working through these questions, you're doing some serious mental muscle-building. You're responsible for your actions, sure, but you can't control others. And hey, that's totally okay. So, keep on journaling, keep on reflecting, and watch yourself grow stronger each day!

AFFIRMATIONS FOR STRENGTH AND RESILIENCE

You've been through a lot, and I want you to know something important – you're stronger and more awesome than you realize.

These affirmations are like little power-ups for your soul. They're here to help you find your inner strength, love yourself more, and build up that resilience that's already inside you. Let's dive into them!

1. **"I am strong, capable, and resilient."** – This is like your personal strength anthem. Say it loud, say it proud. You've got this incredible inner power, and it's time to own it.

2. **"My body is beautiful, and I love it just the way it is."** – Your body has been your buddy through thick and thin. It's time to give it some love and appreciation.

3. **"I forgive myself and accept my feelings."** – Everyone makes mistakes, and that's okay. Forgive yourself like you would forgive your best friend. Your feelings? They're totally valid, no matter what.

4. **"It wasn't my fault."** – Seriously, what happened to you was not your fault. You didn't deserve it, and you're not to blame.

5. **"I have the right to control my body and my life."** – Your body, your rules. Your life, your choices. You're the boss here.

6. **"I am worthy of love, respect, and kindness."** – Yes, you! You deserve all the good things, all the love, all the respect. Don't let anyone tell you otherwise.

7. **"I have the right to be happy."** – Happiness isn't just for others; it's for you too. You deserve to laugh, smile, and have awesome times.

8. **"I deserve safety and peace."** – Feeling safe and at peace is your right. You should feel secure in your world.

9. **"I can create a happy, fulfilling life."** – Your life's story is yours to write, and it can be full of joy, success, and all the things you dream of.

Making Affirmations Part of Your Day

Okay, so why are these affirmations a big deal? They're like daily reminders that help you heal, grow, and find your way back to feeling good about yourself. When you repeat these affirmations, you're slowly rewiring your brain to believe in your awesomeness.

How to Practice Them:

- Stick them on your mirror, so they're the first thing you see in the morning.
- Make them your phone wallpaper.
- Write them in your journal or say them out loud as part of your morning routine.

Remember, healing is a journey, and it's different for everyone. But each time you say these affirmations, you're taking one more step towards feeling stronger, more confident, and totally in charge of your life. Keep going, you're doing amazing!

8

SEXUAL ABUSE

S exual abuse is very serious. Remember to get help from a professional. EFT can greatly help with sexual trauma.

Affirmations can also help but shouldn't be the only thing you rely on for healing.

AFFIRMATIONS FOR EMOTIONAL HEALING

Here are some affirmations to help with healing and self-acceptance:

1. **"My body is mine, and it's amazing."** Remind yourself that your body is your own, and it deserves love and respect.

2. **"I release guilt and shame. They do not belong to me. I am a good, lovable person, no matter what anyone else did to me. I release all shame now."** Let go of any feelings of guilt or shame. They're not yours to carry; they belong to the one who did it to you.

3. **"I am more than what happened to me."** Your experiences don't define your entire being. You're so much more.

4. **"I am worthy of love and respect, always."** No matter what, you deserve to be treated with kindness and respect.

5. **"My feelings are valid and important."** Your emotions matter. It's okay to feel them fully.

6. **"I am strong and resilient."** You've got a strength inside you that's incredible.

7. **"I have the right to be happy and safe."** You deserve a life filled with happiness and safety.

8. **"I am in charge of my life and my choices."** Remember, you have the power to make decisions for yourself.

9. **"I am healing, one day at a time."** Healing is a journey, and it's okay to take it one step at a time.

10. **"I am enough, just as I am."** You don't need to be anything more than what you are right now.

11. **"My past does not determine my future."** You have the power to shape a different, brighter future.

12. **"Every day, I grow stronger and more confident."**
With each day, you're becoming even more amazing.

Remember to say these to yourself, write them down, or even say them out loud. Affirmations can be powerful tools in your journey to healing and self-love.

9

SELF-EMPOWERMENT & SELF-ESTEEM

H ere are some really helpful affirmations to release unfair guilt, shame, blame, and to amp up your self-confidence.

AFFIRMATIONS TO RELEASE SELF-BLAME AND PAIN

If you've been hurt by someone and then told it's your fault, know that it's NOT true. It's unfair blame.

It's crucial to realize that the responsibility for someone's actions lies solely with them, not with those they affect. These affirmations are here to help you release the blame that was wrongfully placed on your shoulders. Repeat each out loud at least 10 times:

1. "Their response is their choice. If they choose an abusive response, that's their choice and not my fault."

    1. "There are always many other ways to respond to a situation, including good, kind, calm, peaceful ways."

    2. "I am only in control of my own reactions, not anyone else's."

    3. "I am not responsible for the actions or mistakes of others. My worth is inherent and independent of their behavior."

    4. "I recognize that my past does not define my future. I am capable of creating a life filled with love and respect."

    5. "I am worthy of kindness and compassion. My experiences do not diminish my value as a person."

    6. "I forgive myself for the times I believed it was my fault. I now know I was doing my best in a difficult situation."

    7. "I deserve to be treated with respect and understanding. My feelings and experiences are valid."

    8. "I acknowledge that I am only in control of my own actions and responses, not those of others. Their choices reflect on them, not on me."

    9. "When someone chooses to hurt me, it is a

reflection of their character, not mine. I am not to blame for their decisions."

10. "I release the burden of others' actions. Their behavior is their responsibility, not mine."

11. "The voices that blamed me were wrong. I now choose to listen to my own voice, one that speaks truth and kindness."

12. "I am strong enough to recognize that another's hurtful behavior is a choice they make, and it is never a reflection of my worth."

13. "I trust in my ability to discern right from wrong. Others' attempts to shift blame do not change the truth."

14. "I am free from the falsehood that I am responsible for someone else's actions. I own my story, not their choices."

15. "I am empowered by the knowledge that I cannot control others, only how I respond and grow from my experiences."

16. "I choose to surround myself with people who acknowledge their actions and respect my boundaries. I deserve healthy relationships."

17. "Every day, I grow stronger in the belief that I am not at fault for the harmful choices of others. This truth sets me free."

These affirmations are designed to help you reinforce your understanding of personal boundaries and responsibility.

Remember, healing from such experiences is a journey, and it's okay to take your time to internalize these truths. You're doing wonderfully by seeking out and using these affirmations. Keep nurturing your inner strength and wisdom.

AFFIRMATIONS FOR SELF-EMPOWERMENT

Here's a list of empowering affirmations to help reclaim your power, your life, and the control of your future:

1. "I am the architect of my life; I build its foundation and choose its contents."
2. "I am in control of my life. I can create any life and future I want. I am now creating a happy, successful, fun life."
3. "Every day, I am growing stronger and more empowered."
4. "I possess the qualities needed to be extremely successful and happy."
5. "My ability to conquer challenges is limitless; my potential to succeed is infinite."
6. "I am in control of my narrative and my life's direction."
7. "I am courageous and stand up for myself and my dreams."
8. "Today, I am brimming with energy and overflowing with joy."

9. "My thoughts are filled with positivity, and my life is plentiful with prosperity."
10. "I am my own superhero. I have the power to create change."
11. "I wake up today with strength in my heart and clarity in my mind."
12. "My fears of tomorrow are simply melting away. I own my future."
13. "I am capable of achieving greatness, and I start that journey today."
14. "Every challenge I face is an opportunity to grow and improve."
15. "I am deserving of my dreams, and I reach for them with confidence."
16. "My voice is important, and my opinions matter."
17. "I am surrounded by abundance and seize the opportunities it brings."
18. "I am a unique individual with so much to offer the world."
19. "I choose to focus on what I can control and let go of the rest."
20. "I am a powerful creator. I create the life I want and enjoy it every day."

Remember, repeating these affirmations regularly can profoundly impact your mindset, empowering you to take charge of your life and embrace the future with confidence and strength.

UNPACKING THE FORGIVENESS KIT

Hey, I totally get it, forgiveness can be super tough, especially if you're still dealing with all those rough emotions. Here's a tip: try EFT (Emotional Freedom Techniques) first to work through the pain and trauma. It's kinda like clearing the clutter before you start redecorating your room. Once the hurt starts to fade, forgiving becomes way easier.

Now, let's talk about some easy forgiveness exercises. These are like your tools for fixing up your emotional space, helping you let go of all that heavy resentment. This way, you can step into a brighter future filled with peace, happiness, and loads of love for the awesome new peeps you're gonna meet and hang with.

1. WRITE A LETTER TO YOURSELF

Here's a simple way to start: Write a letter to yourself. Yep, you heard it right. Pour out all the forgiveness and understanding you can muster. It might feel odd at first, like talking to your reflection, but it's super powerful.

2. POSITIVE MIRRORING

Okay, so here's a super cool trick to help you believe in yourself more, especially if you're feeling down about something personal. It's called Positive Mirroring, and it's kinda like being a cheer- leader for someone else, which in turn helps you too. Here's how it works:

Imagine you're feeling down about something, like maybe you think you're not lovable because of your weight. What you do is to find a picture online of someone who's kinda in the same boat as you. Then, even if you're just chilling alone in your room, start talking out loud to that picture as if you're talking to a real person. Say stuff like, "Hey, you are totally worthy of love just the way you are! Your size? It doesn't define your worth at all!"

Now, here's where the magic happens. The more you keep saying these awesome, positive things to this imaginary person, the more your own brain starts to believe that they're true for you too. You might be wondering, how on earth does that work? Let me explain.

So, imagine inside your brain, there's this little dude who's like a fact checker. His job is to keep all your beliefs in check. The thing is, sometimes he gets it totally wrong, especially if he's holding onto negative untrue stuff like "I'm not worthy of love."

This fact checker is super stubborn and clings to these wrong 'facts,' always finding fake 'proof' to support them. He's like a little warrior, sword in hand, ready to fight off any new ideas that challenge these beliefs.

Now, if you try to hit him with direct affirmations like "I am worthy of love," you're basically picking a fight with him. And let me tell you, it can be tough because this fact checker doesn't back down easily.

But here's a sneaky trick – if you use Positive Mirroring, like telling an imaginary person, "You are worthy of love," you're basically sneaking past this fact checker. He's so busy looking out for direct attacks, he doesn't notice these sneaky side moves. It's like dodging past a security guard while he's busy looking the other way.

By doing this, you're slipping these positive beliefs into your 'brain-computer' without setting off any alarms. And the coolest part? After you do this a bunch of times, your brain starts to actually believe these new, positive things about yourself. It's like updating your brain's software with the best, most positive beliefs. And before you know it, you'll totally believe in your own awesomeness!

So, by doing this Positive Mirroring, you're not only spreading positivity, but you're also rewiring your own brain to believe in your own worth and awesomeness. And that, my friend, is a total win-win!

3. TURN YOUR ABUSER INTO THE VICTIM

Okay, so here's a different way to look at things, especially if you're dealing with all the hurt from an abuser. It's called Positive Projection. It's like flipping the script in your mind and seeing things from a whole new angle. Picture this: your abuser, instead of being this big, scary figure, is actually a victim too. Sounds wild, right? But stick with me here.

A lot of times, people who hurt others have been hurt in the same way themselves. It's like a messed-up cycle. So, the trick to breaking free from all that emotional chaos they caused you is to see them as a victim. Not in a way where you feel sorry for them or anything, but in a way that lets you say, "Okay, I'm done being hurt by you."

Here's how you can do it: First, write down all the nasty stuff your abuser made you feel. Stuff like, "It's my fault they treated me badly; I don't deserve to be treated kindly," or, "My thoughts don't matter."

Then flip it around and write down the total opposite, but in a positive way. Think, "It was never my fault they were mean. I deserve kindness. My thoughts are important."

Now, imagine saying all these positive things *to your abuser*. I know, sounds super weird, right? But as you do this, you start seeing them in a different light. You might even begin to realize that they were acting out because of their own deep issues. Like, maybe they were super pushy about their music taste because they were never allowed to enjoy their own tunes growing up. Or maybe they felt ugly because their dad insulted them, so they kept picking on you and making you feel unattractive.

The wild part is, as you keep doing this, you'll start feeling free from all that pain.

It will crumble away. The crushing pain on your heart will begin to lift and vanish. The burning knots of anger in your stomach will cool off and disappear.

Plus, you'll begin to believe all those good things about *yourself!* It's like breaking a weird dark curse, you know? You might not know everything about your abuser's past, but by flipping the script and seeing them as a victim, you release yourself from their hold in a really weird but effective way.

And that's the real magic – you start healing and believing in your own awesomeness.

372 | JORDAN PHOENIX

4. FORGIVENESS AFFIRMATIONS

Repeat affirmations to forgive yourself and the abuser.

Affirmations for Self-Forgiveness:

1. "I forgive myself and let go of all guilt and shame. I did my best in that moment with what I knew."
   1. "I acknowledge that I handled the situation the best way I could at the time. I forgive myself completely."
   2. "I release myself from the burden of past mistakes. I was doing my best to survive and navigate."
   3. "I understand that everyone makes mistakes, including me. I forgive myself and embrace learning from my past."
   4. "I choose to be kind to myself about the past. I did what I thought was right then, and now I know more."
   5. "I let go of self-blame. My past actions don't define my worth or my future."
   6. "I forgive myself for not leaving sooner. I understand that my fear and uncertainty were real and valid."
   7. "I free myself from the weight of what I 'should' have done. I'm focusing on what I can do now."
   8. "I am more than my past experiences. I forgive myself and grow stronger each day."

9. "Every day, I choose self-forgiveness and self-compassion. I am healing and learning."

10. "I forgive myself and release all guilt and shame now. I did what I could at the time with the knowledge I had. I did my best, and that's enough. I was just doing what I could to handle a difficult situation. I forgive myself. I let it all go now."

Affirmations for Forgiving the Abuser and Letting Go:

1. "I choose to forgive, not for them, but for my peace of mind. I release the hold this pain has on me."

2. "I let go of anger and resentment. Holding onto these feelings only hurts me."

3. "Forgiving doesn't mean forgetting. It means freeing myself from the chains of bitterness."

4. "I forgive as an act of strength, not because what happened was okay, but because I choose to free myself from their hold over my life. I am taking back my power and peace."

5. "Forgiving is my way of saying I am no longer your victim. It does not condone your actions but releases me from the pain they caused. My forgiveness is my path to a life where you no longer have any power to hurt me."

6. "I forgive, understanding that it's a step towards my own healing and freedom."

7. "I release the power that this hurt has over my life. I choose peace and healing."
8. "I acknowledge that forgiving is for me. It's my path to emotional freedom and closure."
9. "I understand that forgiveness is a process, and I am patient with myself as I journey through it."
10. "I forgive, not because it's easy, but because I deserve to move on and live a life filled with joy."
11. "By forgiving, I reclaim my power and my peace. I am not defined by what happened to me."
12. "I let go of the past hurt and embrace a future filled with hope and healing."

Remember, these affirmations are tools to guide you on your journey of healing and self-compassion. They are like small, daily steps towards a more peaceful and empowered you.

PASSING THE TORCH OF HOPE

You've journeyed through the pages, discovered secrets to escape toxic chains, and now you're standing in the light of newfound wisdom. It's your turn to be the beacon for others who are still navigating through the darkness.

By sharing your genuine thoughts about this book on Amazon, you're not just leaving a review; you're guiding lost souls to a safe harbor. Your words can be a signpost for fellow teens searching for a way out of the shadows of harmful relationships.

Your support means the world. It's how we spread the message of hope and healing far and wide. By passing on your insights, you're contributing to a safer, kinder world for teens everywhere.

Thank you for being an integral part of this mission. With each person you reach, you're helping to strengthen the chain of positive change.

Together, we're not just reading about change; we're making it happen.

Jordan Phoenix

Click here to share your journey and light the way for others on Amazon.

https://www.amazon.com/review/create-review/?
ie=UTF8&channel=glance-detail&asin=

CONCLUSION

As we wrap up this bonus Self-Help Guide, I want to leave you with some heartfelt wishes and reminders. You've got an array of tools at your fingertips to continue healing and to protect yourself from future harm. Therapy offers professional guidance and support. Affirmations help reinforce positive self-beliefs. Talking to an AI chatbot like 'Hope' gives you a safe space to express your- self and seek advice, any time you need it. EFT/Tapping is a powerful technique for releasing emotional pain. Journaling lets you reflect deeply on your thoughts and feelings. And critical thinking helps you question and understand your experiences more clearly.

Remember, every step you take is a step towards a brighter, more empowered future. You've got the strength, the tools, and the resilience not just to heal but to thrive. Wishing you all the happiness and health as you continue on your incredible journey. You've got this!

REFERENCES

Agaron, S. (2021, April 16). *Mood Meter: identify and regulate your emotions.* Brain Street. https://shamay.com/mood-meter-app-review/

Aravind, V., Krishnaram, V., & Thasneem, Z. (2012). *Boundary Crossings and Violations in Clinical Settings. Indian Journal of Psychological Medicine, 34*(1), 21– 24. https://doi.org/10.4103/0253-7176.96151

Breaking the Cycle: How to Heal Unhealthy Teenage Relationships. (2023, July 25). ThreePeaks Ascent Residential Treatment Center. https://threepeakstreat ment.com/residential-treatment-for-teens/unhealthy-relationships/

Chaturvedi, S. K. (2023). The Good, Bad and not so Bad of Positive Thinking and Recovery. *Journal of Psychosocial Reha-*

bilitation and Mental Health, 10(2), 129–130. https://doi.org/10.1007/s40737-023-00348-1

Counseling, S. C. (2023, July 20). *9 Ways to Rebuild Self-Esteem After a Toxic Relationship*. Seattle Christian Counseling. https://seattlechristiancounseling. com/articles/9-ways-to-rebuild-self-esteem-after-a-toxic-relationship

Creswell, J. D., Dutcher, J. M., Klein, W. M. P., Harris, P. R., & Levine, J. M. (2013). *Self-Affirmation Improves Problem-Solving under Stress. PLoS ONE, 8*(5), e62593. https://doi.org/10.1371/journal.pone.0062593

15 Tips for Letting Go of a Relationship That Is Not Healthy - GoodTherapy.org Therapy Blog. (2023, November 10). Good-Therapy.org Therapy Blog. https://www. goodthera-py.org/blog/15-tips-for-letting-go-of-a-relationship-that-is-not- healthy-0829167/

15 Tips to Build Self Esteem and Confidence in Teens. (n.d.). Big Life Journal. https:// biglifejournal.com/blogs/blog/build-self-esteem-confidence-teens

Gordon, S. (2021, July 26). *What Teens Need to Know About Boundaries*. Verywell Family. https://www.verywellfamily. com/boundaries-what-every-teen-needs- to-know-5119428

Gordon, S. (2022, September 29). *Benefits of Mindfulness for Kids and Teens*. Verywell Family. https://www.verywellfam ily.com/benefits-of-mindfulness- for-kids-4769017

How do I heal from a toxic relationship as a teenager? (n.d.). Quora. https://www. quora.com/How-do-I-heal-from-a-toxic-relationship-as-a-teenager-2

Kassel, G. (2023, December 7). *9 Signs You're Dating a Narcissist — and How to Get Out.* Healthline. https://www.health line.com/health/mental-health/am-i- dating-a-narcissist

K. (2023, August 18). *20 Simple Ways How to Self-Love After Toxic Relationship.* Pinch of Attitude. https://www.pinchofatti tude.com/self-love-after-toxic- relationship/

K. (2023, July 20). *Online Teen Safety Guide.* StaySafe.org. https://staysafe.org/ teens/

Lonczak, H. S. (2023, October 9). *What Is Gaslighting? 20 Techniques to Stop Emotional Abuse.* PositivePsychology.com. https://positivepsychology.com/ gaslighting-emotional-abuse/

Love is Respect. (2018, September 10). *loveisrespect.org.* Loveisrespect.org. https:// www.loveisrespect.org/

L. (2023, September 4). *Importance of a support system after a toxic relationship - Recovery from Toxic Relationships.* Recovery From Toxic Relationships. https:// toxicrelationshiprecov ery.com/importance-of-a-support-system-after-a-toxic-relationship/

Resilience. (n.d.). https://www.apa.org. https://www.apa.org/ topics/resilience

Self-esteem and teenagers - ReachOut Parents. (n.d.). https:// parents.au.reachout.com/ common-concerns/everyday-issues/self-esteem-and-teenagers

Smith, M. (2024, February 5). *Setting Healthy Boundaries in Relationships.* HelpGuide.org. https://www.helpguide.org/ articles/relationships-communica tion/setting-healthy-boundaries-in-relationships.htm

Social Media and Teen Romantic Relationships. (2019, December 31). Pew Research Center: Internet, Science & Tech. https://www.pewresearch.org/internet/ 2015/10/01/social-media-and-romantic-relationships/

Sun, H., Yuan, C., Qian, Q., Shu-Zhi, H., & Luo, Q. (2022, March 31). *Digital Resilience Among Individuals in School Education Settings: A Concept Analysis Based on a Scoping Review.* Frontiers in Psychiatry. https://doi.org/10.3389/ fpsyt. 2022.858515

Surviving A Relationship Break-Up -Top 20 Strategies. (n.d.). https://www.mcgill.ca/ counselling/files/counselling/sur-viving_a_break-up_-_20_strategies_0.pdf Sweeney, E. (n.d.). *Toxic Relationships and Teenage Mental Health.* The BHS Beat.

https://bhsbeat.org/3124/student-life/toxic-relationships-and-teenage- mental-health/

Teens and social media use: What's the impact? (2024, January 18). Mayo Clinic. https://www.mayoclinic.org/healthy-life

style/tween-and-teen-health/in-   depth/teens-and-social-media-use/art-20474437

Tips for Building Healthy Relationships with Your Teenagers. (n.d.). CAMH. https:// www.camh.ca/en/health-info/guides-and-publications/tips-for-building-   healthy-relationships-with-your-teenagers

Treatment, A. A. (2023, March 14). *Why Healthy Boundaries Are So Important in Recovery.* Ashley Addiction Treatment. https://www.ashleytreatment.org/ rehab-blog/boundaries-in-recovery/

REFERENCES

Academy, V. (2022, September 19). *8 Signs of a Toxic Teenage Relationship.* Venture Academy. https://www.ventureacad emy.ca/troubled-teen-blog/8-signs-of-a- toxic-teenage-rela-tionship/

Agaron, S. (2021, April 16). *Mood Meter: identify and regulate your emotions.* Brain Street. https://shamay.com/mood-meter-app-review/

Aravind, V., Krishnaram, V., & Thasneem, Z. (2012). *Boundary Crossings and Violations in Clinical Settings. Indian Journal of Psychological Medicine, 34*(1), 21–

24. https://doi.org/10.4103/0253-7176.96151

Breaking the Cycle: How to Heal Unhealthy Teenage Relationships. (2023, July 25). ThreePeaks Ascent Residential Treatment

Center. https://threepeakstreat ment.com/residential-treat-ment-for-teens/unhealthy-relationships/

Carl Pickhardt Ph.D. (n.d.). http://www.carlpickhardt.com/parentingarticles.html Chaturvedi, S. K. (2023). The Good, Bad and not so Bad of Positive Thinking and

Recovery. *Journal of Psychosocial Rehabilitation and Mental Health,* *10*(2), 129–130. https://doi.org/10.1007/s40737-023-00348-1

Counseling, S. C. (2023, July 20). *9 Ways to Rebuild Self-Esteem After a Toxic Relationship.* Seattle Christian Counseling. https://seattlechristiancounseling. com/articles/9-ways-to-rebuild-self-esteem-after-a-toxic-relationship

Creswell, J. D., Dutcher, J. M., Klein, W. M. P., Harris, P. R., & Levine, J. M. (2013). *Self-Affirmation Improves Problem-Solving under Stress. PLoS ONE, 8*(5), e62593. https://doi.org/10. 1371/journal.pone.0062593

15 Tips for Letting Go of a Relationship That Is Not Healthy - GoodTherapy.org Therapy Blog. (2023, November 10). Good-Therapy.org Therapy Blog. https://www. goodthera-py.org/blog/15-tips-for-letting-go-of-a-relationship-that-is-not- healthy-0829167/

15 Tips to Build Self Esteem and Confidence in Teens. (n.d.). Big Life Journal. https://

biglifejournal.com/blogs/blog/build-self-esteem-confi-dence-teens

5 Strategies to Cope With Toxic Family Members | Psychology Today. (n.d.). Www.psy- chologytoday.com.https://www. psychologytoday.com/us/blog/in-flux/ 202204/5-strate-gies-cope-toxic-family-members

Forth, A., Sezlik, S., Lee, S., Ritchie, M., Logan, J., & Elling-wood, H. (2021). Toxic Relationships: The Experiences and Effects of Psychopathy in Romantic Relationships. *International Journal of Offender Therapy and Comparative*

Criminology, 66(15), 0306624X2110491. https://doi.org/10. 1177/ 0306624x211049187

'Frenemies' and toxic friendships: pre-teens and teenagers. (2024, March 7). Raising Children Network. https://raisingchil dren.net.au/pre-teens/behaviour/peers- friends-trends/frenemies

Gordon, S. (2021, July 26). *What Teens Need to Know About Boundaries.* Verywell Family. https://www.verywellfamily. com/boundaries-what-every-teen-needs- to-know-5119428

Gordon, S. (2022, September 29). *Benefits of Mindfulness for Kids and Teens.* Verywell Family. https://www.verywellfam ily.com/benefits-of-mindfulness- for-kids-4769017

Helping Your Teen Through an Unhealthy Relationship | Office on Women's Health. (2019, April 30). https://www.women shealth.gov/blog/unhealthy-teen- relationships

How do I heal from a toxic relationship as a teenager? (n.d.).

Quora. https://www. quora.com/How-do-I-heal-from-a-toxic-relationship-as-a-teenager-2

Kassel, G. (2023, December 7). *9 Signs You're Dating a Narcissist — and How to Get Out.* Healthline. https://www.health line.com/health/mental-health/am-i- dating-a-narcissist

K. (2023, August 18). *20 Simple Ways How to Self-Love After Toxic Relationship.* Pinch ofAttitude.https://www.pinchofatti tude.com/self-love-after-toxic- relationship/

K. (2023, July 20). *Online Teen Safety Guide.* StaySafe.org. https://staysafe.org/ teens/

Langdon, A. (2024, January 3). *How Toxic Friendships Can Affect Mental Health.* Harmony.https://www.grwhealth.com/ post/how-toxic-friendships-can- affect-your-mental-health/

Lonczak, H. S. (2023, October 9). *What Is Gaslighting? 20 Techniques to Stop Emotional Abuse.* PositivePsychology.com. https://positivepsychology.com/ gaslighting-emotional-abuse/

Love is Respect. (2018, September 10). *loveisrespect.org.* Loveisrespect.org. https:// www.loveisrespect.org/

L. (2023, September 4). *Importance of a support system after a toxic relationship - Recovery from Toxic Relationships.* Recovery From Toxic Relationships. https:// toxicrelationshiprecovery.com/importance-of-a-support-system-after-a-toxic-relationship/

Navarro, R., Larrañaga, E., Yubero, S., & Víllora, B. (2020). *Psychological Correlates of Ghosting and Breadcrumbing Experiences: A Preliminary Study among Adults. International Journal of Environmental Research and Public Health, 17*(3), 1116. https://doi.org/10.3390/ijerph17031116

REFERENCES | 239

Resilience. (n.d.). https://www.apa.org. https://www.apa.org/topics/resilience

Self-esteem and teenagers - ReachOut Parents. (n.d.). https://parents.au.reachout.com/ common-concerns/everyday-issues/self-esteem-and-teenagers

Smith, M. (2024, February 5). *Setting Healthy Boundaries in Relationships.* HelpGuide.org. https://www.helpguide.org/articles/relationships-communica tion/setting-healthy-boundaries-in-relationships.htm

Social Media and Teen Friendships. (2019, December 31). Pew Research Center: Internet, Science & Tech. https://www.pewresearch.org/internet/2015/08/06/ chapter-4-social-media-and-friendships/

Social Media and Teen Romantic Relationships. (2019, December 31). Pew Research Center: Internet, Science & Tech. https://www.pewresearch.org/internet/ 2015/10/01/social-media-and-romantic-relationships/

Sun, H., Yuan, C., Qian, Q., Shu-Zhi, H., & Luo, Q. (2022, March 31). *Digital Resilience Among Individuals in School Education Settings: A Concept Analysis Based on a Scoping Review.* Frontiers in Psychiatry. https://doi.org/10.3389/fpsyt. 2022.858515

Surviving A Relationship Break-Up -Top 20 Strategies. (n.d.). https://www.mcgill.ca/

counselling/files/counselling/surviving_a_break-up_-_20_strategies_0.pdf Sweeney, E. (n.d.). *Toxic Relationships and Teenage Mental Health.* The BHS Beat.

https://bhsbeat.org/3124/student-life/toxic-relationships-and-teenage- mental-health/

Taylor, C. (2022, March 3). *10 Ways To Set Boundaries With Difficult Family Members.* Taylor Counseling Group. https://taylorcounselinggroup.com/blog/set-bound aries-for-diffi-cult-family-members/

Team, F. (2024, January 31). *Gottman's 7 Principles of Making Marriage Work.* Calgarypsychologist. https://www.flourish psychology.ca/post/gottmans-prin ciples-of-making-marriage-work

Teens and social media use: What's the impact? (2024, January 18). Mayo Clinic. https://www.mayoclinic.org/healthy-life style/tween-and-teen-health/in- depth/teens-and-social-media-use/art-20474437

The Importance of Setting Healthy Boundaries With Your Teen. (2024, March 8). Embark Behavioral Health. https://www. embarkbh.com/blog/the-impor tance-of-setting-healthy-boundaries-with-your-teen/

Thunberg, G. (2022, October 21). *Greta Thunberg on the climate delusion: 'We've been greenwashed out of our senses. It's time to stand our ground.'* The Guardian. https:// www. theguardian.com/environment/2022/oct/08/greta-thun berg-climate- delusion-greenwashed-out-of-our-senses

Tips for Building Healthy Relationships with Your Teenagers. (n.d.). CAMH. https:// www.camh.ca/en/health-info/guides-and-publications/tips-for-building- healthy-relationships-with-your-teenagers

Treatment, A. A. (2023, March 14). *Why Healthy Boundaries Are So Important in Recovery.* Ashley Addiction Treatment. https://www.ashleytreatment.org/ rehab-blog/boundaries-in-recovery/

Understanding Teen Mental Health in the Online Dating Era. (n.d.). Innerspace Counseling. https://www.innerspacecoun seling.com/blog/understanding- teen-mental-health-in-the-online-dating-era

Why Do I Keep Attracting Toxic Partners? | Psychology Today. (n.d.). Www.psychology- today.com. https://www.psycholo gytoday.com/us/blog/women-autism-spec trum-disor-der/202011/why-do-i-keep-attracting-toxic-partners